First published in The United States by Colette Patterns, a division of Colette Media, Portland, OR.

ISBN 978-0-692-57304-4

www.colettepatterns.com
www.seamwork.com

First Edition, 2015

Seamwork

ANNUAL 2015

Welcome to the first annual collection from Seamwork Magazine.

I grew up in the age of zines. Back then, if there was something you were excited about, whether it was teaching people to screenprint in their basements, exploring the world of Star Trek fandom, or writing about your own love life, publication was just a photo copier away. Zines were geeky, they were DIY, and they were highly specific. Most of all, they were a way for diverse and quirky voices to be heard.

Now the web gives us all the chance to be authors, to create our own worlds and explore the tiniest niches of our interests. It was that spirit that brought Seamwork Magazine to life in December 2014. Seamwork is an online magazine that delivers articles and patterns to you every month at Seamwork.com.

We wanted to explore the idea of making your own clothing — admittedly a niche pursuit — in a way we hadn't seen yet. We wanted to talk about clothing from the geekiest technical details to the fascinating history to the wider culture of making all in one place. We wanted to reflect the amazing community of sewists that has sprouted up online in the last five or ten years. Most of all, we wanted to bring together diverse voices to tell stories and share knowledge.

We also wanted to bring some hands-on sewing into the experience, with quick patterns you can make in an afternoon but still learn from. A subscription to Seamwork includes your choice of two of these patterns every month. You'll see many of the patterns from our library sprinkled throughout this book. Our hope is that a steady supply of lovely projects to make and interesting articles will draw more and more people into the world of sewing.

In this first annual collection, we bring together some of our favorite articles from the past year along with new ones that have never been published before. All of these essays, articles, and recipes are appearing in printed format for the very first time. Some people say that the web browser killed the zine, but here we are full circle, with words on paper once again. We couldn't have done it without the web.

Enjoy this collection from some of our favorite voices in the sewing community. You can join us year round at seamwork.com, where you'll find new writing and projects each month. We hope to see you there, bringing your own style and voice.

CONTRIBUTING WRITERS

CHARLOTTE WENSLEY

Charlie Wensley is a Brit sewing up a storm in Brooklyn. She documents her sewing journey on her blog, nobleanddaughter.com.

DEVON IOTT

Devon Iott is a sewing teacher that works for Husqvarna Viking and Pfaff brand sewing machines. She blogs at Miss Make in Nashville, TN with two chickens and a cat.

HALEY GLENN

Haley Glenn is the Managing Editor for Seamwork. She is a professional sewing writer and teacher based in Portland, Oregon.

HEATHER LEWENZA

Heather Lewenza is the designer and blogger behind Closet Case Files. Visit her blog and purchase her patterns at closetcasefiles.com.

JENNY RUSHMORE

Jenny Rushmore is a curvy sewing blogger, who's passionate about helping plus-size women gain confidence through sewing. She blogs at Cashmerette and the Curvy Sewing Collective.

JESSICA YEN

Jessica Yen is a writer, blogger, knitter and sewer based in Portland, OR.

KAT SIDDLE

Kat Siddle is a librarian and fashion school dropout from Vancouver, BC. She blogs about beauty at xovain.com and helps run Our Social Fabric, a textile re-use initiative.

SARAI MITNICK

Sarai Mitnick is the Editor-in-Chief of Seamwork Magazine and Founder of Colette. She often thinks and writes about the way sewing impacts our lives—through body image, identity, and social awareness.

SHAERIE MEAD

Shaerie Mead is a pattern maker and sewing educator living in Los Angeles. You can find her patterns and more info at: https://www.sew-la.com

CREDITS

STAFF

Sarai Mitnick | Editor-in-Chief

Haley Glenn | Managing Editor

Kris Blackmore | Pattern Designer

Wallis Smith-Owens | Patternmaker

Anna Aguirre | Production Assistant

Delaney Matson | Sample Seamstress

Christine Power | Art Director

Taylor Pruitt | Designer

Kenn Wilson | Operations Manager

Meg Stively | Relationship Manager

Sarah Ashlock | Copy Editor

Jessica Yen | Assistant Copy Editor

PHOTOGRAPHY

Christine Power | Photographer

Evie McShane | Assistant Photographer

Christine Power | Art Director

Shayda Rohini | Stylist

Megan Hart | Model

Lynn Denton | Model

Shayda Rohini | Model

Caroline Nuyen | Model

Solanah Cornell | Model

Monica Ninh | Hair/Makeup

SPECIAL THANKS

Laura Row Illustrations

Manor Fine Wares

Sweetheart St. Johns

Shayda Rohini of General Merriment

Karin Dejan

Dawn Moothart

Erica Horton

CONTENTS

LETTER FROM THE EDITOR   04

TUTORIALS   11

Handmade Beauty Recipes   12

Glühwein Recipe   18

A Winter Hat Trio   22

Six Easy Changes: Micro Hacks   32

BEST OF SEAMWORK   45

SEWING LESSONS   45

Coming to Peace   46

Knowing Grandma   50

Finding Me Again   54

TECHNIQUES   59

How to Sew Sweater Knits   60

A Guide to Working on the Bias   70

Sewing Knits Without a Serger   78

Embroidered Snow Flurry   86

TEXTILES   95

The Art of Marbled Fabric   96

Good Silk Hunting   106

Farm to Fabric: The Story of Wool   114

HOLIDAY LOOKBOOK   127

Festive   128

Cozy   136

PATTERNS THAT TEACH

Our signature line of printed and digital sewing patterns, with clear

instructions and classic designs. See what makes Colette the most

popular independent sewing pattern company on the market.

www.colettepatterns.com

TUTORIALS

Let's make something.

Handmade Beauty

Gluhwein

A Winter Hat Trio

HANDMADE BEAUTY

Looking for a unique gift? Try one of these handmade beauty products

CHAI
LOTION BAR

Make a moisturizing lotion bar.

WRITTEN BY: KAT SIDDLE

Frequent travelers will love these flight-friendly solid body lotions. Scented like a warm cup of spiced chai, these lotion bars are a cinch to make and very easy to customize. You can use different molds to change the size or shape, or fiddle with the base oil and fragrance to create a perfectly personalized gift. Because these bars do not contain water, they'll last for a long time. (To be on the safe side, sterilize your equipment before making them, and use up the bars within six months).

Good packaging will turn these convenient lotions into a truly luxurious gift. Candy foil makes a good oil-proof wrapper, but I think that tins are best for storing the bars securely. Buy your tin before you make the bars: it's easier to find a mold that fits a tin than vice-versa. Vintage tins are lovely, but you can also buy plain tins and customize them with paint or washi tape.

I used a variety of silicon cooking and baking molds to make my lotion bars. My favorite bar—a palm-sized dome—was created using a silicon egg poacher! Silicon muffin cups, ice cube trays, and cake pop pans are all excellent options.

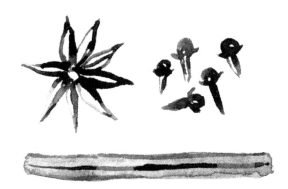

YOU'LL NEED:

- ▨ 1/3 cup beeswax pellets

- ▨ 1/3 cup shea butter

- ▨ 1/3 cup coconut oil or any oil of your choice

- ▨ 30 drops chai-blend essential oil. You can create your own by combining cardamom, cinnamon, clove, and ginger essential oils, but for most people, it will be less expensive to buy a pre-blended mix.

- ▨ A double boiler, or a large glass measuring cup and a small-to-medium-sized pot.

- ▨ A sterile spoon

- ▨ A silicon mold. This recipe makes about 1 cup of lotion. I prefer to make 3–4 small bars of lotion, but you can make them any size. Make sure your mold is completely clean and totally dry.

HOW TO:

1. Combine the beeswax, shea butter, and coconut oil in the double boiler and heat on medium low until all the wax is melted. If you're using a measuring cup and pot, fill the pot halfway with water. Combine the top three ingredients in the measuring cup. Place the measuring cup in the pot, making sure no water spills into the cup. Heat the pot on medium-low until all the wax is melted.

2. Remove the double boiler/pot from the heat. Add 30 drops of essential oil (you can add a little more if you like). Gently swirl the oil and wax mixture with a sterile spoon to ensure that it's evenly mixed.

3. Pour the mixture into the mold(s). The bars won't shrink or grow as they dry, so you can fill the molds to the top.

4. Let the lotion bars cure for 12 hours at room temperature.

5. Remove the bars from the molds. This can be tricky. While they usually come out of the mold easily, you want to avoid touching them as much as possible (you don't want to give a gift with fingerprints on it!) Make sure your hands are clean, watch out for long nails, and work in a cool room if possible. I found that popping the bars directly into their tins worked best.

SPRUCE AND PINE
HAIR POWDER

Add texture to second day hair.

WRITTEN BY: KAT SIDDLE

I love hair powders and dry shampoo. A quick application of hair powder make unwashed hair look fresh and clean, and it adds volume and grip, making hair easier to style. It works especially well on fine, straight hair that tends to be oily. (If you have dry, curly, or kinky hair, skip ahead to Floating Rose Hair and Body Oil).

Most dry shampoos are aerosol sprays that produce a lot of needless waste. Non-aerosol options exist, but they're so simple that it's crazy not to make your own for a fraction of the price. Natural hair powders are often a mix of cornstarch and a mineral called silica. In this recipe, I've substituted clay powder for silica. This makes a light-colored powder that should work on most hair colors. If you're making it for someone who has very dark hair, you can add 1/8 tsp. of cocoa powder to deepen the color (and give it a rich chocolate scent).

The trick to good hair powder is to find ingredients that are as fine-ground as possible. If one of your flours is unpleasantly gritty, leave it out! Replace it with an equal amount of cornstarch, arrowroot powder, tapioca, or rice flour. A smooth texture is more important than exact proportions.

YOU'LL NEED:

- [ ] 2 tbsp. cornstarch or arrowroot powder

- [ ] 1 tbsp. rice flour or tapioca flour

- [ ] 1/2–1 tsp. kaolin clay powder or French green clay

- [ ] 1–3 drops of essential oil. I used 1 drop of spruce oil and 1 drop of pine, but you can use any skin-safe oil you like.

- [ ] A small, narrow-necked bottle. Tiny liquor bottles work especially well. Make sure your bottle is clean and completely dry on the inside.

- [ ] Clean paper, like parchment or copy paper.

- [ ] A small bowl

- [ ] Non-metal fork, chopstick, or whisk

- [ ] A small funnel

HOW TO:

1. Cover your work surface with clean paper (not newspaper). This might get messy!

2. Combine the cornstarch, clay, and rice or tapioca flour in a small bowl. Add essential oils. Stir with a small non-metal fork, chopstick or whisk until the oil is evenly dispersed. If the powder looks clumpy, add a little more clay.

3. Use a small funnel to pour the powder into your narrow-necked bottle (or make a funnel from a piece of paper).

TO USE:

Shake a small amount (1/8–1/4 tsp.) of hair powder into your palm. Using clean fingertips, massage the powder into the roots of your hair until it disappears. If you have shorter hair, dust both hands with powder and run them through your hair.

FLOATING ROSE
HAIR AND BODY OIL

Make a super easy moisturizing oil.

WRITTEN BY: KAT SIDDLE

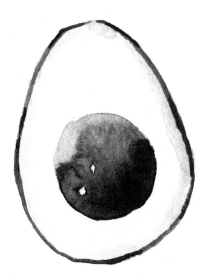

This floral hair and body oil is as simple as it is pretty, and takes minutes to make. Avocado oil can be a little hard to find, but it's worth the trouble. This highly moisturizing oil absorbs into skin quickly and has very little smell. Used sparingly on hair, it tames flyaways and adds shine.

YOU'LL NEED:

- A clear bottle with a dropper top
- Enough avocado oil to fill the bottle
- 5–7 whole dried rosebuds (make sure they're small enough to fit inside the bottle without being crushed)

HOW TO:

1. Make sure the bottle is clean and completely dry on the inside.

2. Carefully drop the rosebuds into the bottle.

3. Fill the bottle to the top with avocado oil.

TO USE:

Rub 1–2 drops between your hands and run your hands through the mid-lengths and ends of your hair.

Or, apply 2–3 drops to dry skin or nails.

Kat Siddle is a librarian and fashion school dropout from Vancouver, BC. She blogs about beauty at xovain.com and helps run Our Social Fabric, a textile re-use initiative.

GLÜHWEIN

A recipe for the perfect holiday "glow"

WRITTEN BY: SHAERIE MEAD

Before moving to California and opening Sew L.A., I was a baker for many years. The holidays were always a flurry of activity as I baked fruitcakes (the real kind, with liquor), cookies, gingerbread, panettone, and stollen for customers, friends, and family. I would always have some mulled wine simmering on the stove, wafting the scents of spices and orange through the entire house to add to the seasonal mood.

Fast forward ten years, and I'm lucky if I have time to bake even one round of cookies for my loved ones! But I ALWAYS have time for hot wine with spices in it, and my favorite variety is the traditional German glühwein ("glow" wine—you'll soon see why). My husband and I are lucky enough to live close to a real German biergarten, the Red Lion Tavern. We started going there regularly for the great beer and delicious food, and when the holidays rolled around they added this wine to their menu. One mug and I was hooked. We also had three Sew L.A. holiday parties in a row at the Red Lion, and intrepid YouTube searchers can find a very drunken rendition of "Bohemian Rhapsody" sung by the entire staff.

Glühwein is usually served at German Christmas markets to keep the shoppers warm as they go from stall to stall. These markets have been around since the 1400s, so they have had plenty of time to perfect their recipes! If you are lacking holiday spirit, all you have to do is look up pictures of these charming markets online to really get into the mood. And certainly, the delicious smell of warming glühwein will also do the trick!

GLÜHWEIN:
Serves four normal people or two people who really like Glühwein.

YOU'LL NEED:

- ½ cup sugar, agave, or a blend
- ¾ cup water
- 1 orange
- 1 lemon
- 1 small cinnamon stick
- 6 cloves
- Small piece of nutmeg
- 1 inexpensive bottle of merlot, cabernet sauvignon, or any dry red wine
- ¼–½ cup brandy or rum

HOW TO:

1. To make the syrup, place sugar or agave and water in a large saucepan. On low heat, stir to dissolve.

2. Peel the orange and lemon in large strips with a sharp knife or vegetable peeler. Try to avoid as much of the white pith as possible. Place peel in saucepan.

3. Juice the orange and lemon and add the juice to saucepan.

4. Add cinnamon stick, cloves, and nutmeg to the saucepan. Stir well.

5. Simmer on low for ½ hour.

6. You can strain out all the chunks or leave them in. Whichever you decide, after the syrup has simmered, add the wine and brandy or rum and heat until warm. Ladle into mugs.

GLÜHWEIN PARTY:

Serves 24-32

Don't be afraid to experiment with spices and citrus! This is a traditional recipe with as many variations as you can think of. There's no right way to do it. I use cinnamon, cloves, and nutmeg because that's what I have; some fancy recipes throw in 2–3 cardamom pods and/or 1–2 star anise. I DO recommend organic citrus, as you'll be infusing the peel, and you don't want any nasty chemicals in there.

Wine-wise, red's the rule but within that, go for a variety you would normally drink. The wine should be drinkable on its own, but don't waste really good wine on this. The spices and heat will render the expense meaningless. I have seen versions of this recipe that don't add any other liquor (the more the merrier, in my opinion), and also recipes that add brandy, rum, kirschwasser, and even amaretto. And here's my secret: I make a double batch of the syrup portion and keep half in the fridge for when I need some glühwein RIGHT NOW. Because that happens.

If you would like to make this for a party, you can prepare the syrup in advance and transport it in mason jars. Set up a crock pot, and monitor the temperature closely. Depending on your pot, you may have to set it for warm to heat everything up, then turn it off for a bit so it doesn't start boiling.

YOU'LL NEED:

- 4 cups sugar, agave, or a blend
- 6 cups water
- Peel & juice of 8 oranges and 8 lemons
- 6 cinnamon sticks
- 20–30 cloves
- 1 nutmeg, cracked into pieces
- 8 bottles dry red wine (I cannot think of a better use for "two buck chuck" from Trader Joe's)
- 2–4 cups brandy or rum

HOW TO:

1. Bring all syrup ingredients to just a boil, then simmer on low for ½ hour.

2. Cool syrup.

3. Divide into 4 wide mouth quart size mason jars (or similar sturdy transportation vessels).

4. When ready to make glühwein, dump one of the mason jars into your crock pot along with 2 bottles of wine and ½–1 cup brandy or rum.

5. Heat till warm, then keep warm and covered.

6. As it is consumed, add syrup and wine in the same proportion to keep it full. You'll be surprised at how fast you go through all 8 bottles.

PROSIT!

Shaerie Mead is a pattern maker and sewing educator living in Los Angeles. You can find her patterns and more info at Sew-LA.com

A Winter Hat Trio

Make a stylish and warm beanie.

WRITTEN BY: DEVON IOTT

Make one of these hats (or all three!) to keep your noggin nice and toasty when the weather gets cold. The Basic Slouchy Beanie is your classic slouchy hat—wear it uncuffed for maximum slouch, or cuff the brim back for a closer fit. The Fringe-Pom Hat starts the same way but adds a chunky self-fabric pom-pom, and the Ski Patrol Hat has a classic winter look with fleece lining, earflaps, and chin ties.

MEASURING AND CUTTING NOTES

Since knits have different stretches and all humans have different heads, you'll be cutting the fabric at a custom measurement based on your head size and fitting as you go. Measure the circumference of your head at the point where the bottom of a hat lands when you wear it. We will refer to this number as H.

22"

BASIC SLOUCHY BEANIE

Materials: ¾ yard medium weight jersey, or similar knit fabric

Cutting: Cut one 23" long x H" wide

In general, most hats will be most comfortable with negative ease of 1"–3". By cutting the fabric as wide as your head circumference and then using a ½" seam allowance, you'll be starting out with negative ease of 1". You can then take it in from there if necessary.

Keep your H number handy, as you'll be using it when cutting your fabric. When cutting all hat pieces, make sure that the edges with the H measurement are in the more stretchy direction on the fabric (most often perpendicular to the selvage).

Unless otherwise indicated, for all seams use either a serger or a narrow zigzag stitch and a ½" seam allowance.

SEWING:

01 Fold fabric in half, right sides together, lining up 23" edges. Stitch together along 23" edge.

22" x 23"

02 Turn the tube halfway so that raw edges are aligned. With the fold at the bottom, carefully try on the hat to check the fit. Adjust the seam if necessary.

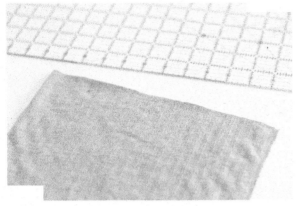

03 Once satisfied with fit, return the tube to the wrong side out. At the top open end, mark the center of the edge, then mark the center of each half. Make all marks ½" in from raw edge. Do not include the seam allowance of the already sewn edge when measuring.

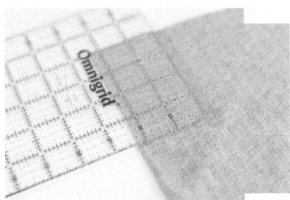

04 Mark 4" down on fold edge.

05 Draw a curved line from the mark at the fold edge up to top of the nearest mark at raw edge. Blend each edge smoothly into the mark, so you don't create points when sewing.

06 Pin layers together and stitch along line. Stop at the mark and backstitch. Don't sew all the way to the edge of the fabric at the top. (Note: even if you have a serger, steps 6–12 should be sewn on a regular machine).

07 Repeat on other side, again remembering not to include the seam allowance when marking and sewing.

08 Pull apart both sides of the tube and fold the top, so that you are bringing the sides of the remaining opening together and aligning the raw edges. Look at the edges from above—you should be lining up the two seams you just sewed, and all the folds should be making a "+" sign.

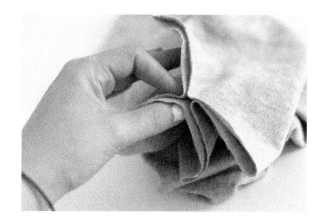

09 Fold three of the folds back, so you are looking at one of the unsewn folds. Mark 4" down from the top on the fold edge.

10 Draw a curved line between the marks like you did before, blending the ends to make a smooth curve.

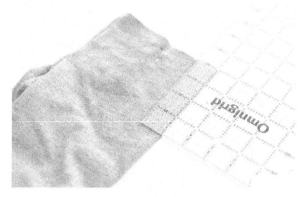

11 Stitch along the line, making sure you're only sewing through two layers and all other folds are out of the way. Start the seam exactly on the mark or one stitch in front of it; you want to avoid sewing into all the layers of folded fabric.

12 Repeat with other unsewn fold.

13 Trim seam allowances down to ¼".

14 Repeat with the other open end of the tube, but leave a 3" opening in one of the seams.

15 Turn the tube right side out and push out all edges. Fold the seam allowance of the opening to the inside and pin.

16 Edgestitch along opening to close.

17 Push the lining (edgestitched) side into the other side. Wear your new hat as-is for a slouchy look, or fold the edge

FRINGE-POM HAT

Materials: ¾" yard medium weight jersey, or similar knit fabric

01 Follow the cutting instructions for Basic Slouchy Beanie sewing steps 1–2. Return tube to wrong side out.

02 Mark a line 3" from one open end.

03 Using a rotary cutter or scissors, cut through both layers up to the line in ¼" increments. Continue until the entire edge is cut.

04 Trim off the fringe with the seam allowance in it.

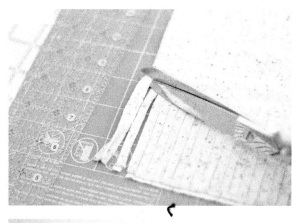

05 Repeat on other open end.

06 Turn the tube halfway, so that the wrong sides are together and the fringes are aligned.

07 Cut a piece of fabric that is 1" x 8". Gather the fringe end of hat together at the base of fringe and tie the fabric tightly around it with knot at the hat seam allowance. Trim the knot ends to ½".

08 Try on the hat and trim any fringe as necessary to get a round pom-pom shape.

SKI PATROL HAT

Materials: ⅜-yard medium-weight jersey or similar knit fabric for exterior; ⅜-yard furry fleece for lining (make sure it stretches); two 18" pieces thick yarn; ⅛" fusible tricot interfacing; pom-pom (optional)

Cutting: Exterior and fleece: one 12" long x H" wide; two 4.25" long x 4.75" wide

01   If your exterior fabric is on the lighter side (e.g., T-shirt weight), fuse some knit/tricot interfacing to the wrong side.

02   Fold exterior ear flap in half vertically (lining up 4¼" edges). Trim bottom half into a circle shape as shown.

03   Trim a fleece lining piece to match.

04   Trim ¼" off the whole curved edge of the exterior earflap. This will create a small border of fleece once you sew the pieces together.

05   Place one piece of yarn centered on the bottom edge of the exterior earflap as shown. Stitch across the end at ¼" seam allowance.

06 Pin the exterior and fleece right sides together, aligning the entire curved edge. You will need to stretch the exterior slightly to fit the fleece.

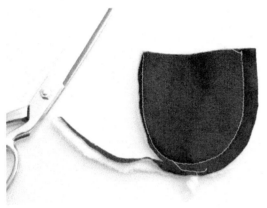

07 Stitch around the edge with a standard machine. Trim the seam allowance to ⅛". If your yarn frays easily, zigzag a few times over the end of it within the seam allowance.

08 Turn the right side out and press with low heat. Repeat to make a second earflap.

09 Fold the main exterior piece right sides together and stitch along the 12" edge. Repeat with the fleece. Try it on to check the fit.

10 Turn the fleece tube right side out. Place earflaps to tube, fleece sides together, with raw edges of flap and tube aligned. Pin so that center of earflap is 4½" from the seam on tube. Pin at the stitching line (½" from edge) and carefully try on the fleece to check earflap placement. Adjust if necessary.

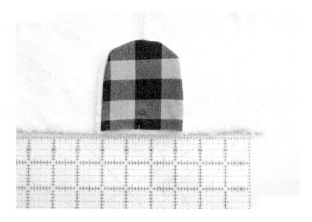

11 Stitch across both earflaps at ¼" seam allowance.

12 With fleece right side out and exterior wrong side out, slide the exterior around fleece and line up the bottom (earflap) edges. The earflaps should be sandwiched in between, and the fleece and exterior tubes should be right sides together. Pin all the way around the edge.

13 Sew all the way around pinned edge. This seam must be very stretchy, so a good option is a triple straight stitch on a regular machine. You can also serge, but depending on your fleece choice, the earflaps might be a bit bulky for a serger.

14 Flip the fleece away from the exterior to create a long tube. Turn the wrong side out and finish both open ends by following steps 3–17 of Basic Slouchy Beanie. Be careful that the yarn doesn't get caught in any of the seams, and leave a larger opening for turning.

15 Once finished, trim the yarn ties to the desired length, knot edges, and fray the yarn to create a tassel. *Optional: attach a yarn pom-pom to the top of the hat.*

Devon Iott is a sewing teacher that works for Husqvarna Viking and Pfaff brand sewing machines. She blogs at Miss Make in Nashville, TN with two chickens and a cat.

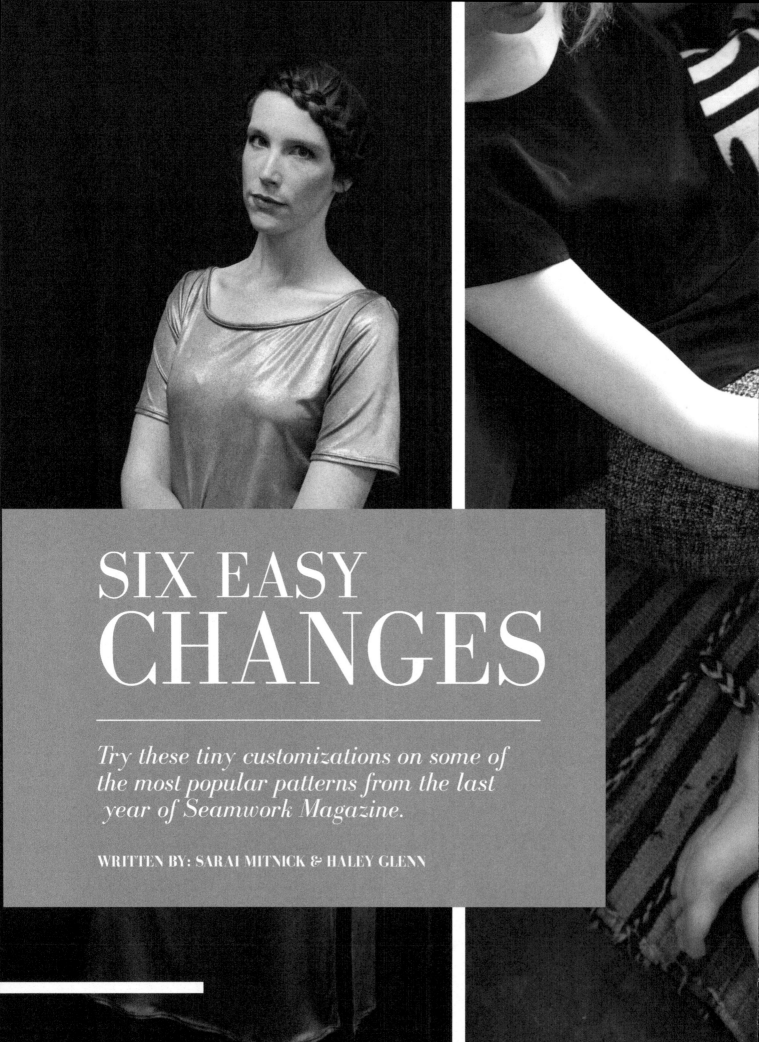

SIX EASY CHANGES

Try these tiny customizations on some of the most popular patterns from the last year of Seamwork Magazine.

WRITTEN BY: SARAI MITNICK & HALEY GLENN

One of the greatest things about sewing is the opportunity to change just about everything. Not only do you get to choose your pattern and fabric, you can also make tiny adjustments to get exactly the style you want. Sometimes even the tiniest tweaks can make you feel like you're wearing custom clothing.

To celebrate the first year of Seamwork patterns, we came up with six simple and quick changes you can make to get more out of three of our favorite patterns. See if any of these easy changes gives you a fresh perspective on an old favorite. You can download these patterns at Seamwork.com.

SAVANNAH

The Savannah camisole just might be the most effortless Seamwork pattern. Its ability to work as a stand-alone garment or as a layering piece is unparalleled. Dress Savannah up by using a simplified bias neck finish or by lengthening it into a slip dress.

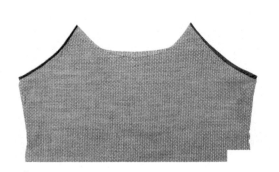

SAVANNAH WITH BIAS FINISH

01 Cut a piece of bias tape the length of your underarm seam. Unfold the first fold in the bias tape and look at the remaining two folds—one is smaller. Unfold the smaller fold and with right sides together, align the raw edges of the bias tape and underarm seam.

02 Stitch the bias tape to the camisole following the crease closest to the edge.

03 Refold the bias tape so that the unsewn edge wraps around the raw edge to the wrong side of the garment.

04 Edgestitch along the inner edge of the bias tape through all the layers.

05 Repeat with the other underarm seam.

06 Cut a piece of bias tape that is a total of 12" longer than the back neckline.

07 Find the center of the bias tape and back bodice. Open the bias tape and pin the centers together, with the raw edges aligned and the right sides together.

08 Stitch in the first crease along the entire edge to attach the bias tape to the bodice, just like you did on the underarms. Do not edgestitch.

09 Repeat to attach the bias tape to the front in the same manner. Don't edgestitch yet.

10 Open the bias tape all the way and pin right sides together, being careful not to twist the straps.

11 Try on the camisole and adjust the straps if necessary. Stitch the straps together and trim the excess to ¼". Gently press the seam open.

12 Refold the bias tape on the creases all the way around neckline. Repress if necessary, especially where straps are joined.

13 Starting on the back bodice, edgestitch along the bias tape all the way around the dress, stitching along the back bodice, first strap, front bodice, and second strap. Execute with extra care while stitching the straps.

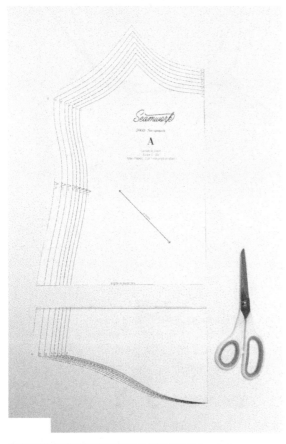

SAVANNAH DRESS

01 Determine how much you would like to lengthen your Savannah. You can lengthen Savannah by as much as you like. If lengthening Savannah much more than 8", consider sizing up and cutting on the length of grain.

02 Cut on the lengthen or shorten line.

03 On a separate piece of pattern paper draw two parallel lines, the distance between these two lines should be the amount you would like to lengthen.

04 Draw a third line perpendicular to the other two. This will act as a continuation of your center front.

05 Align the upper and lower portion of your cut camisole pattern with the lengthening lines and grainline continuation line. Tape to secure.

06 Use a ruler to redraw the lengthened portion of the side seam.

07 Cut and sew according to the pattern instructions.

MESA

Mesa is an effortless pullover dress that is perfect for mixing and matching through all seasons. Mesa's simple shape and fitted style makes it easy to dress up or down. Elevate this chameleon of a dress by applying a clean finished bind to the neck, or lengthen Mesa by turning the split hem into deep side slits.

LENGTHEN MESA DRESS

01 Determine how much you would like to lengthen your Mesa.

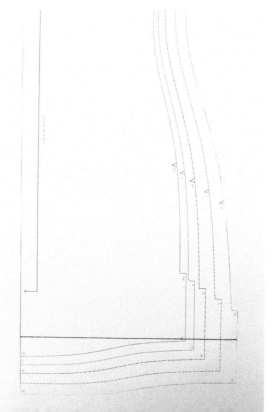

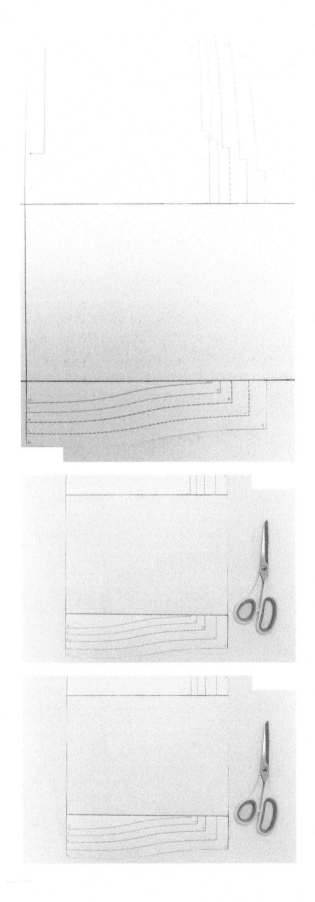

02 Draw a line perpendicular to the grainline below the split hem notch. This is your lengthen line.

03 Cut along the drawn line.

04 On a separate piece of the pattern paper, draw two parallel lines. The distance between these two lines should be the amount you would like to lengthen.

05 Draw a third line perpendicular to the other two. This will act as a continuation of your center front.

06 Align the upper and lower portion of your cut lengthen line with drawn continuation lines and lengthening lines. Tape to secure.

07 Use a ruler to redraw the lengthened portion of the side seam.

08 Cut and sew according to the pattern instructions.

MESA WITH A CLEAN-FINISHED BINDING

01 Cut the Mesa dress according to the pattern instructions, omitting the neckband.

02 Sew one back dress to one front dress, with right sides together at just one shoulder.

03 Cut a strip of knit fabric 1½" wide. This strip should be longer than the opening you are sewing it to.

04 Fold the binding in half lengthwise, with wrong sides together.

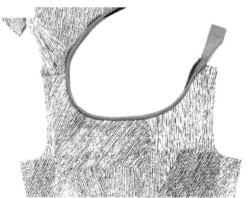

05 Align the binding with the raw edge of the neckline. With right sides together, stitch the binding to the edge using a serger or your favorite stretch stitch.

06 With right sides together, stitch the remaining seam closed, also closing the binding. Reinforce the seam with a bar tack.

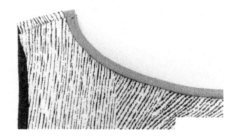

07 Turn the binding to the inside of the garment, folding along the seamline.

08 Edgestitch the band in place using a straight stitch.

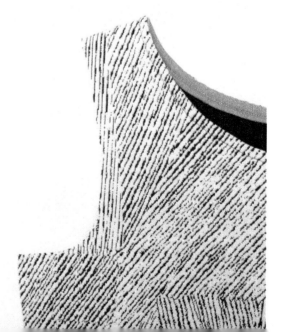

MOJI

When it comes to pants, it doesn't get much more stylish than Moji.
The relaxed peg fit make these pants our favorite secret pajamas.
Step up the comfort of these pants by swapping the drawstring
waist for an elastic option. Adding elastic to the cuff also adds to
Moji's laid-back appeal.

ELASTIC WAIST MOJI

01 Cut the Moji pants according to the pattern instructions using your desired fabric. Sew and attach the pockets, and assemble front and back legs, joining at the crotch.

02 Assemble and attach the waistband to the pants, do not edgestitch the waist casing closed.

03 Edgestitch, catching the bottom fold on the inside of the waistband and leaving a 3" hole at the center back.

04 Wrap 1¼" elastic around the high hip to determine a comfortable length. Cut the elastic and insert into the waistband using a bodkin.

05 Join the two edges of elastic, taking care not to twist it. Close the hole in the waistband using a straight stitch.

CROPPED ELASTIC CUFF MOJI

01 Cut version 2 of the Moji pants.

02 Draw a line 2" from and parallel to the un-notched edge of the front cuff. Cut along this line, discarding of the strip cut from the un-notched edge. Repeat on second front cuff and both back cuffs.

03 Sew pants according to pattern instructions.

04 With right sides together, stitch one front cuff piece to one back cuff piece along the short edges. Press open. Finish the top and bottom edge of the cuff using a serger or zigzag stitch.

05 Turn the un-notched edge under ½" toward the wrong side. Press. Repeat steps 5–6 on the second cuff.

06 With the right side of the cuff facing the wrong side of the pant leg, align the notches and side seams. Stitch along the bottom of the cuff.

07 Turn the cuff to the right side of the pants. Press the cuff up.

08 Wrap ¾" wide elastic around ankle to determine desired length. Add ½" for overlap. Cut elastic.

09 Topstitch the upper edge of the pant cuff, leaving a 2" gap at the inseam.

10 Using a bodkin, insert the elastic into the cuff. Join the short edges of elastic. Stitch the unseen gap at the inseam closed.

11 Repeat steps 7–11 for the second cuff.

 Sarai Mitnick is the Editor-in-Chief of Seamwork Magazine and Founder of Colette. She often thinks and writes about the way sewing impacts our lives - through body image, identity, and social awareness.

 Haley Glenn is the Managing Editor for Seamwork. She is a professional sewing writer and teacher based in Portland, Oregon.

SEWING LESSONS

Stories on how sewing influences our lives.

Coming to Peace

Knowing Grandma

Finding Me Again

COMING TO
PEACE

*Sewing has radically changed my body
image in ways I never could have imagined.*

WRITTEN BY: JENNY RUSHMORE

L ike so many women, I've struggled with body image since I was a child: As a four-year-old hearing that my tummy stuck out too much in ballet class; as a fifteen-year-old wearing a skirt with a painful waistband for years, because I could not fit into my school uniform; and as a twenty-something struggling to convince myself that someone would overlook my appearance and go on a date with me. If you told me when I started sewing five years ago that it would fundamentally change how I perceived myself, I never would have believed you. Though my curvy body hasn't changed, my perceptions and attitude towards it have, quite radically.

First, it freed me from the tyranny of clothes shopping. Knowing you may not fit into the largest size is no fun. There are few things more disheartening than always reaching for the hanger at the back of the rail, asking the shop assistant if a shirt comes in a bigger size, or getting stuck trying

It wasn't my body that wasn't fitting the clothes—it was the clothes that weren't fitting my body!

to squeeze yourself into pants you really, really wish fit over your hips.

In fact, it wasn't until I stopped shopping for clothes that I realized how I felt excluded and judged for not being a "normal" size. It turns out that it wasn't my body that wasn't fitting the clothes—it was the clothes that weren't fitting my body! Now, I decide what I want to wear and make it in my size, and it fits 100% of the time. Who cares where I am in the size range of that store's customers, or if Anthropologie deigns to fit this mighty bosom? Freedom from having to meet someone else's standards is so sweet.

Once I stopped trying to meet someone else's arbitrary size chart, I was able to start paying real attention to my body in a neutral, objective way. Learning about the blocks

The sewing community has been fundamental in my attitude shift. Replacing Photoshop-enhanced images with curvy women of all shapes and sizes, smiling in their crop tops, and swirling in their circle skirts has made me realize that I truly am just like everyone else.

used in ready-to-wear clothing and sewing patterns was an "aha!" moment for me. Of course I don't fit into the clothes in all stores! No one does! Even if you have the same measurement as someone else, everyone's weight is distributed in a slightly different way.

The joy of sewing is that a pattern can be easily adjusted with no value judgment.

It's really hard to have a non-skewed sense of what you look like when you're constantly reminded that you're plus-size. But if you measure your waist, and it's 40"; you just make a 40" skirt. It's a straight-forward equation, and there's really no point in pretending you're a different size or judging the number. You start to understand that the dimensions of your body are just impartial guides to help you make clothes that fit. The more you measure, the more those measurements just become numbers. Suddenly my bust wasn't a "problem," it was just a measurement to help me make something awesome that will fit well.

On a practical note, learning to fit was key. In my frustration and desire to wear a certain size, I wore ill-fitting clothes all my life, with waistbands cutting in and button plackets gaping, causing all sorts of lumps and bumps. Lo and behold, once I made things that fit me, I not only felt more comfortable but also looked so much better! Fitting is a never-ending learning exercise but even beginners start to see the results quickly. Psychologically, it can be hard to size up in clothes from a store (and a lot of the time many of us don't have that luxury as we're already the biggest size), but I've found it so much easier to make the right size when I'm sewing, which always looks so much better.

Finally, the sewing community has been fundamental in my attitude shift. Replacing Photoshop-enhanced images with curvy women of all shapes and sizes, smiling in their crop tops, and swirling in their circle skirts has made me realize that I truly am just like everyone else. It's so much fun to see a photo of a

woman looking fantastic in an outfit and then realize that I can recreate that look and look just as awesome.

There's so much positivity and confidence to be had, if you just know where to look. The support and community from actively engaging in the blogosphere has also been fantastic. The plus-size blogosphere is rapidly growing, with sites like the Curvy Sewing Collective (which I co-founded) gaining new readers every week. If you want to trade tips on getting just the right button-down pattern or help on how to expand a waistband, there are now many places to go.

So thank you, sewing. Not just for my new (and constantly growing) wardrobe, but also for the peace that has come with a positive body image and my ridiculously big grin every time someone takes a photo of me twirling in a garment made just for me, by me.

 Jenny Rushmore is a curvy sewing blogger, who's passionate about helping plus-size women gain confidence through sewing. She blogs at Cashmerette and the Curvy Sewing Collective.

"*From the age of about 10 to about the age of 33, I thought I temporarily looked like this and any day now, it would change. And it's only been very recently that that's changed.*"

-Jenny Rushmore

JOIN THE CONVERSATION:

www.seamwork.com/radio

Stories about designing, making, and wearing your own clothing

KNOWING GRANDMA

Across generations and language, craft can bind us closer to those we love.

Illustration by Laura Row

My paternal grandmother was the only grandparent I really knew. The others passed away before I was old enough to know them. Grandma taught me to knit, and it was through crafting that we developed a bond that lasted well beyond that first lesson.

At 12, I'd already picked up crochet, embroidery and sewing, but knitting still eluded me. Mom pointed at the brightly striped afghans in our living room, all of which had been knit by

WRITTEN BY: JESSICA YEN

Grandma, and suggested I ask her to teach me.

Grandma lived an hour and a half away by plane or seven hours by car, so I only saw her a couples times a year. She usually greeted us by clasping our hands and asking about our grades. Then she patted our hands in encouragement before returning to conversation with the adults. Grandma spoke mostly Chinese, which also limited our interactions. My request surprised her, but she agreed.

She brought straight knitting needles and some leftover acrylic yarn to the next family event. We huddled on a couch away from the rest of the family, where she showed me how to cast on. Grandma had the gnarled, swollen hands of someone who'd worked hard her whole life. While my index fingers rested flush against the aluminum needles, arthritis warped her knuckles so badly that her fingertips bent off at right angles. As we worked through knits and purls, I shyly asked Grandma about her childhood.

Grandma was born in China in the 1920's. I didn't yet know enough Chinese history to realize that the first 25 years of her life were defined by war. There were warlord turf battles (her grandfather once ran China's second largest triad), a protracted civil war between Communists and Nationalists, then the Japanese invasion and World War II. Grandma

In my 20's I began sewing garments, and our conversations expanded to include clothing.

had lived through all of this, but she just waved me off with a curt, "You don't want to hear about that; those were hard years." Still, it was the first real conversation we'd had. I sensed that she, too, felt the generational, linguistic, and cultural chasm between us. I kept bringing knitting projects to family events so that I'd have an excuse to spend time with her. Knitting became my vehicle to develop a relationship with my grandmother.

After a while, Grandma began revealing small tidbits about her life in China. As a child, she and her girlfriends sometimes knit in class, projects sandwiched between desk and lap as they feigned interest in the teacher's lectures. She laughed as she said this, delighted at the memory that drifted to the surface

after all these years. Often she only had enough money for one sweater's worth of yarn. The following year she ripped out last year's sweater and reused it in a new design. She waved her crooked hands as she said this, and I imagined a pullover transforming into cardigan, crew neck to v-neck, ribbed hem to folded hem.

If I asked Grandma point-blank about herself, she usually demurred. But if I waited until we perched side by side, our hands companionably occupied with needles and yarn, the stories bubbled up spontaneously. She told me about fleeing cross country at the age of 13, her mother and younger cousin in tow, when the Japanese invaded. She told me about raising seven children on her husband's modest salary. There was just enough food money to moisten rice with bacon oil and serve it with a few pickled vegetables. She waited until everyone else was done before she ate, standing at the kitchen sink and scraping rice out of the bottom of the pot.

Usually it was just the two of us. I began to tell her about my college major and my various jobs. My cousins were all headed for medical school, dental school, or law school,

I felt sure that the knitter in Grandma still existed, even if she only appea- red for a minute or two at a time.

but I'd chosen Chinese Literature because I wanted to connect with my cultural heritage. Grandma was the one person in my life who anchored my connection to my roots, and she didn't judge my decisions the way the rest of my relatives did.

In my 20's I began sewing garments, and our conversations expanded to include clothing. Grandma, it turned out, had a real eye for fashion. She was a no-nonsense woman who sewed Dad a suitcase full of indestructible plaid shirts when he left for college, but she enjoyed my whimsical tastes. "What did you make this time?" she'd ask, clucking appreciatively at my Kelly green shift

dress with giant eyeglasses printed on it. We were an island of two as we scrutinized flat felled seams and piped necklines.

"Much nicer than what I made in the factory," she'd sigh once we finished dissecting the garment's innards. Another wartime story revealed through our mutual love of clothing and craft.

In the final years of her life, Grandma suffered a series of heart attacks and strokes. Knitting was the last thing she could do. My aunt bought her size 13 needles and Aran weight yarn and Grandma knit up scarf after scarf, glad to still be useful. We snatched up those scarves and paraded them in front of her. Grandma pretended not to notice, but a pleased smile played on her lips.

Her last stroke came in the spring of 2013 and robbed her of control over most of the right side of her body. Knitting was now impossible. She often refused to speak English with

the hospital staff. Then they'd leave and she'd stage whisper to Dad and me, "That's not true! I ate well yesterday."

"You need to cooperate with them!" Dad said. Grandma said nothing, but she had a glint in her eye. She was slowly preparing to leave us, and she was less and less interested in playing by someone else's rules. All our exchanges now took place in Chinese. As a child, I'd sometimes found Grandma's Chinese hard to understand. She spoke with a heavy Hubei accent that favored the second and fourth tone, and she sometimes did things like pronounce the word for "medicine" like the one for "friend." After all these years, understanding Grandma came naturally.

After a particularly disheartening visit to the nursing home, when even the subject of knitting and clothing failed to rouse much interest from Grandma, I laid in bed and cried. Grandma was dying and I couldn't do anything about it. I'd tried every trick I could think of, even pulled out a magazine to compare notes on which Oscar dresses we liked best and why, but nothing worked. Grandma was tired. On some level, I couldn't blame her. She'd had a hard life, and there was so little left for her now.

So I did the only thing I could think of. I knit her a pair of socks. I selected a self-striping yarn filled with her favorite colors—reds, purples, and pinks—and used a pattern that constructed the socks on the bias. I felt sure that the knitter in Grandma still existed, even if she only appeared for a minute or two at a time, and I believed she'd appreciate these touches.

When I showed Grandma the socks, she gave me the widest smile I'd seen in months. When I slipped them on her feet she kept staring down at them in wonderment, and then staring up at me in apprecia-

tion. Dad feared the nursing facility would lose the socks, so every time I left I slipped them into my purse. I always felt guilty taking them from her, but her eyes inevitably lit up the next time she saw them, which was a small consolation.

I brought Grandma's socks to her funeral. Rigor mortis had stretched her features into a grotesque caricature of the woman I'd known; as long as I kept my eyes on her face, I could pretend this had happened to someone else. But the minute I looked at her hands with those joints bent at odd angles from one another, it finally hit me that she'd passed. I cried and fled the open casket, then came back and cried some more.

"I love you Grandma," I whispered as I slipped the socks into the casket. The wool/nylon blend held up well through multiple washings, the colors still cheerful after all this time. To me, they represented Grandma's mix of hard pragmatism and personal style.

There was so much more that I wished I'd asked Grandma, but the reality is that she was a hard woman to know. Crafting created the opportunity for a relationship, and I'm grateful for the memories I have. I heard stories she'd never shared with anyone else. When I was with her, I didn't worry about the family rivalries swirling around me. I had Grandma. The rest didn't matter.

We're approaching the one year anniversary of Grandma's passing. In my stash sits a wool/nylon sock yarn in reds, pinks and purples. It's the sister skein to Grandma's. When I'm ready, I'll make myself a matching pair.

 Jessica Yen is a writer, blogger, knitter and sewer based in Portland, OR.

FINDING ME AGAIN

Sewing and Motherhood.
WRITTEN BY: CHARLIE WENSLEY

Roughly two years ago at about 2 a.m., I was feeding my four-week-old baby and randomly scrolling through my phone to keep myself awake, when I happened upon a sewing blog. The first series of the Great British Sewing Bee had just finished. I found the blog written by Tilly Walnes and my interest was piqued. Pretty soon I had set up a Bloglovin' account and was obsessively reading more and more sewing blogs each feeding time.

I have sewn in sporadic patches since I was twelve, but by the time I had my second child, I probably hadn't touched a sewing machine in ten years. My life prior to having children was about my job, commute, friends, and social life in London. My identity and sense of self was tied up in those things. Despite seeing myself as a creative person, I never did anything creative. I worked. Hard. I went out and I went on vacation a couple of times a year. That was it. But that all stopped when I had my children. We moved out of London, away from friends. I wasn't working or going out at all; I was left floundering. After the initial all-consuming joy of having babies, I was left with this big hole, that, as much as I adore my children, couldn't be filled by caring for them alone.

I had defined myself for such a long time through my job and my life in London, and suddenly it wasn't there anymore. I didn't know who I was or who I should be; my whole sense of myself had been completely upended. Was this it? How was I going to fulfill all of the things I had planned for me, all the possible versions of my life, all the possible me's, if this was it?

Illustration by Laura Row

> *Sewing is enabling me to create my own Charlotte-shaped mold, and my confidence is slowly growing.*

You only have to look at the number of sewing blogs and sewing-related businesses run by stay-at-home moms to realize that I am probably not alone in these feelings. At that time, I wasn't in a position to think proactively about how to tackle these feelings and was diagnosed with post-natal depression. I was referred for therapy, and one of my objectives as part of that was to force myself to spend some time each day doing a hobby or something that I get satisfaction from. Sewing was the only thing I could think of that I had the tools for already and meant I could still be in my house with the kids.

So I started making. Little things at first: baby pants, a gathered skirt for my daughter, cushions, but then as I read more and more blogs, I found the world of indie sewing patterns and off I went. And then we upped sticks and moved across the Atlantic and I discovered New York City's Garment District and, well, that was enough to ignite a full blown sewing craze blaze!

Sewing has become hugely important to me. If I don't sew for a couple of days, I can feel myself getting antsy and irritable. I have found something I love to do; something that is a representation of my abilities above caring for and loving my children. Something that taps into a long suppressed creative side, something that allows me to do things how I think they should be done.

Sewing helped restore my sense of self.

Sewing helped restore my sense of self. In fact, I think it has not just restored it, but it is actually helping me understand who I am, what I want from my life, and what is important in a way I didn't know before.

A large part of this is due to the sewing community. Here, I feel like I

have found my tribe: Those folk, who are part geek, part introvert, part perfectionist, part fashion fiend; people who are trend aware, detail-focused, style conscious, anti-conformist, vocal, passionate, tactile, and creative. I see myself in the people I have met in the virtual sewing community and have realized it's OK to be one of those folk. Although this little corner of the world isn't what I used to aspire to, it's a happy, healthy, productive, inspiring, and supportive one.

I have always been ambitious and competitive and always wanted a high-flying career, but never quite got there. This was the source of much disappointment, feelings of failure, being envious of my friends who seemed to have it, and bitterness towards my employers whom I blamed for my stagnation. Paradoxically, that person, that person who worked so hard, that person whose identity was her job, never felt like me; I always felt like an imposter—as if I was going be exposed at any moment for not knowing what I was talking about. Contorting myself to fit the corporate mold and then a prescribed mother mold hammered my confidence.

Sewing is enabling me to create my own Charlotte-shaped mold, and my confidence is slowly growing. Sewing rules are there for interpretation and misinterpretation. A pattern is a starting point rather than a manifesto. A seam finish is my decision. I can express my personality and style through the sewing decisions I make, and I feel happy with what is emerging.

It is hard to describe, but this flexibility with the rules and how one interprets them has opened my eyes and given me more confidence in my own way of doing things, not only as a person who sews, but also more widely in my life. Gradually, I don't feel like an imposter or that I have to fit a certain mold, or subscribe to a certain parenting style. I can decide my own way of being a mother, my

own way of being a role model to my children, rather than constantly benchmarking it to others or worrying I shouldn't do something for fear of being judged. I have new confidence in my way being the right, or at the very least, an OK way.

This confidence is bolstered by feeling like I have found something I am good at (or so I'm told), that I have something to contribute and I actually know what I'm talking about. The actual creative act of sewing, the constant learning and the huge sense of productivity that are byproducts fulfill my need not to stagnate, to be industrious and to do something that is just for me when life with two small kids can often not feel like my own.

All of these revelations stem, I believe, from the meditative and methodical process of sewing. Losing myself in a particularly tri cky sleeve insertion, or repetitively doing the same movement over and over on a long hand-stitched hemline provides

not only escapism, but also time and space to contemplate.

So, whilst the first few years of motherhood have been both a joy and a challenge, and I think depression is something I will always live with, these two life-changers have lead me to sewing, which in turn is taking me down a path where I have found community, creativity, clarity, and confidence. Where it ultimately leads for me, in terms of my career, I still don't know, but with this new appreciation of who I am and my identity outside of my job and my role as a mother, I'm OK with that.

 Charlie Wensley is a Brit sewing up a storm in Brooklyn. She documents her sewing journey at on her blog and Instagram @charliewensley

YOUR WEEKLY

SNIPPETS

SEWING TIP

KEEP CONE THREAD ORGANIZED

Keeping your cone thread neat and untangled can be a hassle. Small spools of thread feature a "thread catch" that allows your to secure the loose tail of thread. This helps to prevent a tangled thread monster in your notions box.

Try using a box cutter to cut a small notch at the top of your cone thread. This small trick is a simple, but effective way of keeping your cone thread tidy and organized.

Sign up for Snippets to receive weekly sewing tips right to your inbox.

Subscribe now at www.getsnippets.com

TECHNIQUES

Learn as you sew.

How to Sew with Sweater Knits

A Guide to Working on the Bias

Sewing Knits without a Serger

Embroidered Snow Flurry

HOW TO SEW WITH
SWEATER KNITS

Whip up a warm wool cardigan without spending months knitting.

WRITTEN BY: SARAI MITNICK

The Oslo cardigan in a textured wool knit

Sweater knits come in a range of styles & textures.

Sweater knits often have pronounced texture, from nubby surface texture to cables to lacy eyelets.

A s beautiful as hand knit sweaters are, there's no doubt that only the most dedicated and productive knitters can make enough to stay warm all winter. Knitters and non-knitters alike can create their own sweaters in just a couple hours when sewing with sweater knit fabrics.

The Oslo cardigan can be constructed in just a few hours and can be made in bulky wool knits, merino jersey, cotton jersey, or just about any other knit fabric you can think of; but sewing with sweater knits gives it that truly handmade look. Not only that, but sweater knits offer tremendous variety. Read on to learn how to construct a huge variety of looks from one pattern.

SWEATER KNITS DEMYSTIFIED

The term "sweater knit" can be used to describe a number of fabrics used to sew sweaters. Generally, they tend to resemble fabrics that are knit by hand, with a great deal of texture or fuzziness. The knit patterns also tend to be open, with thicker individual yarns than what you might see in other knits, such as jersey.

Sweater knits are by no means the only type of knits that can be used to sew a sweater. Depending on the final look you want, wool or cotton jersey, rib knits, novelty knits, and even lingerie fabrics can be used to construct sweater-like projects. But sweater knits will get you closest to the look you might imagine when you picture a cozy sweater.

Sweater knits come in a range of styles and patterns. Some are quite loose, made with fine gauge yarns in lacy eyelet patterns. Sometimes these types of knits are also referred

The Oslo cardigan in Italian wool sweater knit. Not all sweater knits have an open structure; some are quite dense.

to as "crochet knits" in stores because of their lacy look, though they are usually not crocheted. Other sweater knits have the loose look, but without lacy patterns. Still others are more densely knit, but made with fuzzy or textured yarns. Depending on which you use, you may want to vary your sewing techniques.

Stretch mesh has the weight, invisibility, and hand you need when stabilizing sweater knits.

THE MAGIC OF MESH

If you've sewn with woven fabrics in the past, you're likely most familiar with fusible interfacings. Interfacing adds additional stability, crispness, and weight to an area of your garment. When it comes to sewing soft sweaters, these qualities aren't always what you're going for.

Still, there are times when a little extra stability can come in handy with these loose fabrics. For those situations, try using a stretch mesh fabric as interfacing. These fabrics are most often found in the lingerie section of the fabric store. They work well because they stretch along with your knit fabric, are light enough to prevent added bulk, and are nearly invisible.

Stretch mesh can be found in the lingerie section and can be used to add stability, cover raw edges, or change the hand of your sweater knit.

Look for a mesh that closely matches your main fabric, or choose one that comes close to your skin tone. Here are a few ways you can use mesh along with your sweater knit to make sewing easier:

- Use it as a sew-in interfacing for any area that needs a little more structure.

- Sew strips of mesh into seams to stabilize them and keep them from stretching out over time.

- Use strips of mesh to bind the raw edges of your seam allowance and prevent fraying.

- Cut squares of mesh and baste them behind buttonholes for added stability.

- Use mesh to bind the raw edge of a hem before turning and stitching.

Six

SWEATER KNIT TIPS

01

Cut extra seam allowance for open or lacy knits that are prone to fraying or unraveling.

02

Use a stretch needle to prevent puncturing the fabric.

03

Minimize pressing, so you don't flatten the texture with heat and steam. The more texture your knit has, the more careful you should be.

04

When pressing is needed, apply just the tip of the iron to the seam. Keep the entire iron plate from contact with the fabric.

05

Stabilize areas that are prone to stretching, such as shoulders, by sewing in clear elastic.

06

Wash finished garments carefully by hand, avoiding heat or agitation.

An open knit such as this eyelet can unravel if not cut and sewn with care.

SEWING WITH LACY OR OPEN SWEATER KNITS

If the sweater knit you've chosen for your project is an open knit or lacy, follow a few extra guidelines to prevent excessive fraying.

Cutting

Begin by cutting extra seam allowance with your pattern. Most patterns designed for knits have seam allowances of only 3/8 inch. This may be too narrow for lacy knits, because the holes created by the lace can easily go beyond the seam allowance and cause fraying. Depending on the looseness of the knit, use a seam allowance of 1/2 inch to 3/4 inch.

Stitching seams

Stitch the seams of the sweater with the zigzag stitch of your sewing machine, setting the length to 2.00mm and the width to 1.5mm. This narrow zigzag will allow your seams to stretch, preventing them from popping when the sweater is worn. Because the stitches of a serger are narrow, the zigzag stitch is better suited for these types of sweater knits.

Sew the seam allowance with a zigzag stitch, then finish the raw edge with a serger or another row of stitching.

Follow these guidelines to keep your lacy knit from fraying.

Lacy knits like this one can be used to create lightweight layering sweaters.

Pattern shown: The Oslo Cardigan.

Once your seam is sewn, finish the raw edges. You can either use a serger at this point, or sew another row of zigzag stitches along the raw edge to secure all the threads and prevent further fraying.

Hemming

To hem an open lacy knit, first finish the raw edge. You can do this by binding it with a strip of stretch mesh, or try sewing a band of stretch lace around the edge. Stretch lace can often be found among the lingerie fabrics at your local sewing store, and will stretch along with the garment while remaining inconspicuous.

Once the edge is finished, turn the hem up and sew invisibly by hand using a catch stitch.

With dense sweater knits, seams can be sewn with a serger if desired.

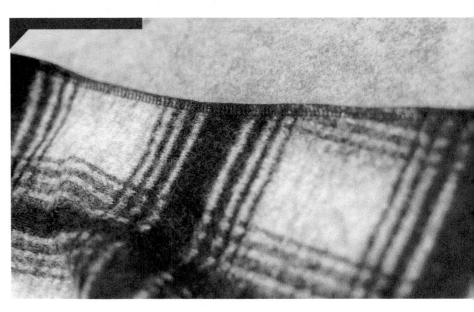

SEWING WITH DENSE SWEATER KNITS

Dense sweater knits need less special handling, but can still be prone to fraying.

To sew seams, you may use a serger if you choose. Be sure to test sew a scrap of fabric before constructing your entire garment to make sure your fabric will hold up. Alternately, zigzag stitch seams on your sewing machine, as instructed for the open knits. If you sew with a zigzag, be sure to finish the raw edges afterward, just as you would with an open knit, by zigzagging or serging the raw edges to prevent fraying.

To hem a dense knit like this, you may use the same hand sewing techniques as you would for an open knit, or you can turn the hem and use a twin needle to stitch. A twin needle creates two parallel rows of stitching and allows the hem to stretch when worn.

Sarai Mitnick is the Editor-in-Chief of Seamwork Magazine and Founder of Colette. She often thinks and writes about the way sewing impacts our lives - through body image, identity, and social awareness.

" *Dense sweater knits need less special handling.*

You may use a twin needle to create a stretchy hem.

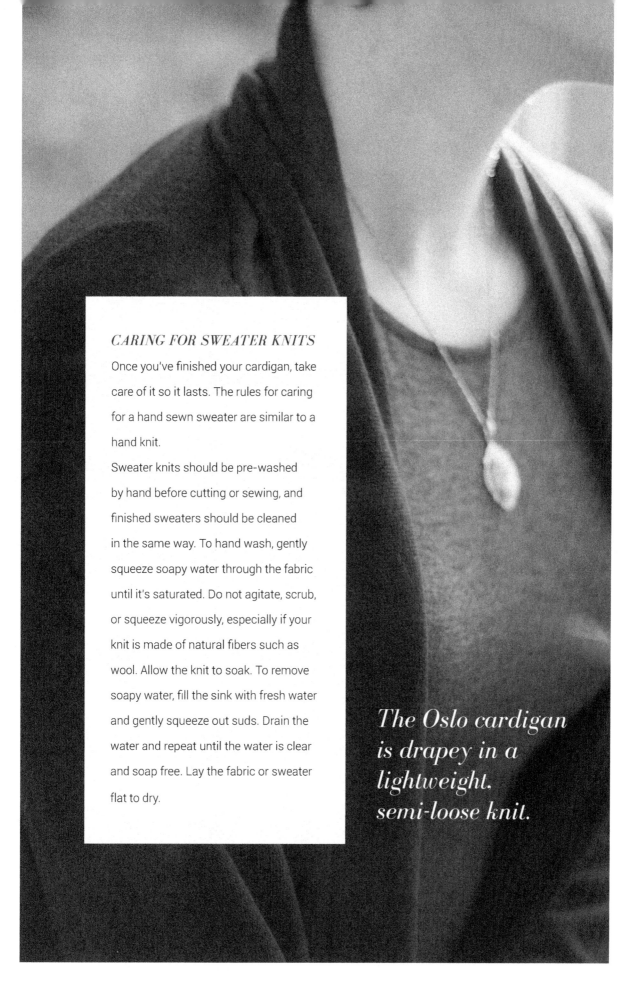

CARING FOR SWEATER KNITS

Once you've finished your cardigan, take care of it so it lasts. The rules for caring for a hand sewn sweater are similar to a hand knit.

Sweater knits should be pre-washed by hand before cutting or sewing, and finished sweaters should be cleaned in the same way. To hand wash, gently squeeze soapy water through the fabric until it's saturated. Do not agitate, scrub, or squeeze vigorously, especially if your knit is made of natural fibers such as wool. Allow the knit to soak. To remove soapy water, fill the sink with fresh water and gently squeeze out suds. Drain the water and repeat until the water is clear and soap free. Lay the fabric or sweater flat to dry.

The Oslo cardigan is drapey in a lightweight, semi-loose knit.

A GUIDE TO WORKING
ON THE BIAS

Tips and tricks for gorgeous flowing garments.

It is impossible to contemplate the bias cut garment without imagining flowing gowns and delicate intimates, but this technique does not need to be reserved for only the most sumptuous of projects. You can bring a bit of everyday luxury to the simplest garment just by cutting it on the bias. Bias cut garments are figure flattering and hang delicately.

WRITTEN BY: HALEY GLENN

" You can bring a bit of everyday luxury to the simplest garment just by cutting it on the bias.

The first time I attempted to work on the bias many years ago, I was trying to make a tie. I chose a sumptuous, striped silk remnant, went to the thrift store and bought a tie to rip apart and blindly jumped in. Out of pure frustration, I gave up on the project. Fast-forward a year, and I decided that it was time for me to give bias a second shot. I made a simple woven t-shirt out of a solid linen, and I was in love.

This experience taught me a few things about the process of learning new techniques, as well as working on the bias specifically. I learned that balancing familiar skills with new techniques is the best way to master new skills. This method has helped me tackle techniques that challenge me.

Vintage lingerie often employs a bias cut to create a clinging silhouette.

This dress by designer Betsey Johnson uses sheer bias cut silk over a stretch lining to create a feminine, comfortable party dress.

Since then I have made many garments using the bias grain of fabric, and have found the key techniques that give professional results. Working on the bias doesn't have to be intimidating. By simply making a few mindful choices and practicing some additional care, you can be on your way to becoming the next Madeleine Vionnet (or at least her fabulous modern protégé).

WHAT IS THE BIAS?

The true bias refers to the 45 degree angle that intersects the warp (length of grain) and the weft (cross grain) of a woven fabric. Every piece of woven fabric has two true biases perpendicular to each other. Though technically any diagonal cut that is not on the lengthwise or crosswise grain is a bias cut, in conventional usage when people refer to a bias cut they are usually talking about the true bias.

The Savannah camisole is cut on the bias for an easy flow and comfortable stretch that skims the body.

The bias of woven fabric offers both stretch and malleability, and can easily be molded to take shape. These properties are both the advantage and disadvantage that most experience when working on the bias. Though it offers a forgiving fit, the instability of the fabric can be difficult to work with.

BEFORE YOU SEW

Start off on the right foot by choosing an easy fabric and cutting accurately.

Start Simple

When braving your first attempt at sewing a garment cut on the bias, keep it simple. Choose a pattern that has details that you are comfortable sewing. Keep in mind that the inherent stretchy nature of bias means that it is best not to choose a fussy garment with eight darts. The malleable nature of the fabric itself will provide shaping and ease.

Choosing Fabric

Choose a fabric in a solid or all over print to start. When working on the bias for the first time, you should avoid stripes and plaids that need to be matched and super slinky fabrics, like silk charmeuse or chiffon. Start out with uncomplicated styles and easy fabrics and build on your existing skills. Try beginning with a cotton lawn, plain weave linen, or a wool challis. These are excellent options for your first time sewing a bias garment.

Fabrics to always avoid are heavy weight canvases, twills, and stretch fabric. Fluid and slippery fabrics, such as rayon, slinky silks, and synthetics should be avoided for your first few bias projects, but can serve as good goals to work towards. These simple choices will allow you to focus on the new techniques you are learning while working on the bias.

Cutting and Layout

Take your time when cutting a bias cut garment. If even slightly off the true bias, your garment can pull unattractively on the body. Cutting your fabric single layer is an absolute must. Prepare your pattern accordingly by making sure all pattern pieces are full, and not cut to be placed on the fold. If the

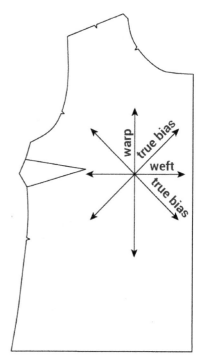

The bias can refer to any diagonal grainline, but it typically refers to the true bias, which runs 45 degrees from the warp or weft.

Cut all pattern pieces on a single layer of fabric rather than a fold.

back biases perpendicular to each other. This results in a balanced garment. If the garment has center front and back seams, the direction of the bias should alternate around the body.

Stabilize

When working on the bias, many (if not all) of your cut edges should be stay stitched. For best results, make sure to sew 1/8" in from your seam allowance. Use fusible knit interfacing to stabilize areas where |closures are to be added. Knit fusible has a small amount of give that accommodates the stretch of the bias. You can also cut woven fusible interfacing on the bias. Another area that can benefit from interfacing is the neckline.

pattern piece is intended to be cut on the fold, cut one half and flip over the center line to cut the other side.

Use a rotary cutter if this is a skill you are confident in. Normally when using a rotary cutter, I favor pattern weights, but pins can offer more control. Using a combination of both can be very helpful. If you choose to use fabric shears and you find the fabric to be unwieldy, place a layer of tissue beneath your fabric to assist you in cutting; this lends added stability through both the pinning and cutting process. When pinning, be sure to pin through all layers (tissue, fabric and pattern), as this will yield the most stable results.

When considering the layout of your garment it is important to remember that every fabric has two true biases, each perpendicular to the other. When the front and back of a dress are cut on parallel biases, the dress has a tendency to twist around the body. Instead, cut the front and

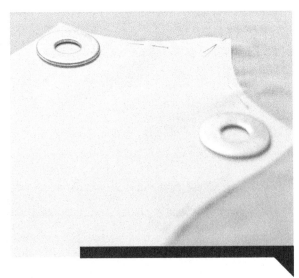

A combination of pins and pattern weights can help you control your pattern.

Cut pieces so that the bias grainlines meet in opposite directions. This will help avoid twisting on the body as the garment is pulled in a circle.

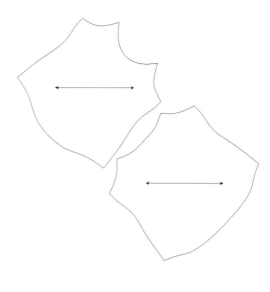

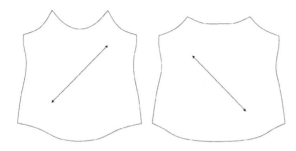

When laid on fabric, the pattern pieces will face different directions.

Use a very narrow zigzag seam to allow the stitching to stretch along the body.

STITCHING A BIAS GARMENT

Seam Construction

Bias cut garments have the tendency to stretch over time and during wear. If the seams do not stretch with the fabric, this can cause the seams to bust. The trick is to create a seam that will stretch along with your garment. This is where a very narrow zigzag stitch can be superior to a standard straight stitch. Set your machine for zigzag stitch, with a length of 2.5mm (or 2mm for finer fabric) and a width of 0.5mm. This will allow the stitching to move and stretch in the same way that a bias cut garment would.

Use a gentle touch when handling your fabric. Avoid pulling or allowing the fabric to stretch out of shape, and support fabric rather than letting it hang.

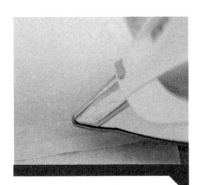

Don't let your iron pull the fabric out of shape. Use an up and down pressing motion.

Use a light hand

Many sewists, especially beginners, tend to pull the fabric as they sew. Whether this is pulling towards you and against the feed of the sewing machine or pulling the fabric from behind the machine and away, this will stretch out your seams. The result will be rippled seams and a stretched out garment.

Instead, use a light hand and support the weight of your fabric. I had a tailoring teacher once tell me "in sewing, you have to know when to use your baby hands and when to use your trucker hands". This, my friends, is definitely an occasion to use the former. A light touch will take you far!

Press, don't iron

When pressing seams, it is always best to press using an up and down motion with the iron rather than ironing in a back and forth movement. Ironing can stretch and distort the grain of the fabric. This becomes particularly problematic when working on the bias.

Using the correct pressing tools is also vital. On shaped seams, use your pressing ham and a seam roll or sleeve board when pressing in tight places. These tools will help you to maintain the shape of your garment as you sew.

Store flat

While your project is in the process of becoming a garment, store the pieces flat. This is handy for two reasons. First, you will reduce the need to iron stubborn wrinkles out, avoiding any unnecessary stretching. Second, storing your project

Shape seams by pressing them over hams and seam rolls.

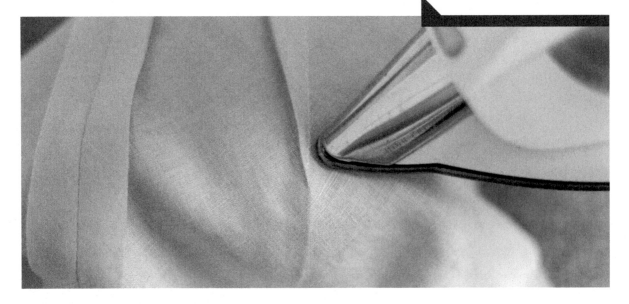

flat instead of hanging also helps reduce stretching.

Nothing can ruin the elegance of a garment quite like an uneven hem. Avoid this by hanging your garment overnight before hemming. This will allow the fabric to naturally settle. Afterward you can trim any drooping areas and hem according to pattern specifications. Hanging your garment from a dress form is another option when allowing the fabric to settle. This can be especially useful with a garment with a lot of seaming and shaping. The dress form can help to mold the dress, as well as allowing the hem to settle.

One of the key things I preach to all of my sewing students is a steady progression of skills. Remember that sewing should be fun! Choose projects that allow you to focus on a few new skills at a time. You will absorb more knowledge this way and enjoy yourself much more. Sewing on the bias for the first time can be tricky. Remember that challenging yourself is a terrific way to learn, but like anything moderation is key.

Haley Glenn is the Managing Editor for Seamwork. She is a professional sewing writer and teacher based in Portland, Oregon.

Before hemming, allow the garment to hang and stretch.

SEWING KNITS
WITHOUT A SERGER

Simple tips for using your home sewing machine to sew knit fabrics.

WRITTEN BY: HALEY GLENN

As a sewing teacher, I have become acutely aware of a paradox that exists in the sewing community. Though the average person's wardrobe consists mostly of knitwear, the majority of seamstresses sew almost exclusively with woven fabric. This could be attributed to the misguided notion sewing knits requires a serger. This is absolutely false! Though a serger makes the assembly of knit garments much faster, they are a costly addition to your sewing arsenal and are not imperative. The following is a guide to sewing knits on your home sewing machine.

HANDLING

The stretch and resilience of knit fabric makes them such a joy to wear. Knits move with our bodies and active lifestyles, giving us room

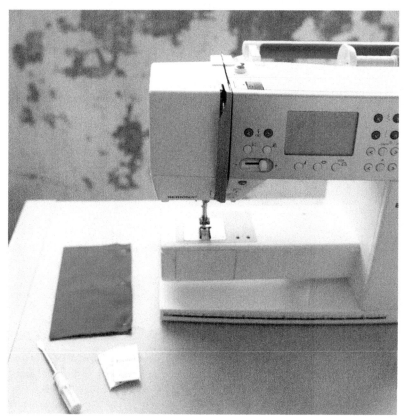

to grow and move. These qualities are what make knits unique, but also require us to handle them in a different manner.

PREPARING YOUR SEWING MACHINE

Making a few simple adjustments on your machine before sewing will help you get off on the right foot when working with knits.

NEEDLES

Correct needle choice is essential to successfully sewing knit fabrics. Universal needles have a slightly rounded tip and are intended for switching between wovens and

TIPS AND TRICKS FOR HANDLING KNITS

- Use ballpoint pins to avoid damaging knit fabric while cutting and sewing.

- Always reserve a few scraps to test your needle and machine settings. Test stitches with the stretch of the fabric and against it. Both directions of the fabric will behave differently and may require slightly different settings. Take note of these variations and store with your project as you work.

- Do not stretch as you sew or resist the feed of your machine by pulling the fabric toward or away from you.

- Support the weight of your project while you sew. Do not let it fall to the ground as it passes through your sewing machine. This will stretch your fabric and put unnecessary stress on your sewing machine. Instead, position your sewing machine so there is plenty of space for your fabric to be supported behind and to the left of your sewing machine.

- If some stretch occurs during the sewing process, hover your iron approximately 1" above the stretched seam and apply steam. The heat and moisture of the steam will help to shrink the seam back to its intended size and shape.

The location of this dial or lever can vary from machine to machine. Refer to your machine manual to learn more about the presser foot pressure on you sewing machine.

On the left, a seam sewn with help of a walking foot, on the right, a seam sewn without.

knits. Though a universal needle can sometimes work for knits, it is always best to exchange your needle with a needle that is specifically intended for the task of sewing knit fabrics.

A needle with a rounded tip, commonly called a ballpoint needle is optimal. A ballpoint needle gently pushes through fabric, rather than piercing the fibers, helping to avoid runs and tears. A standard ballpoint needle is ideal for most knit projects. Ballpoint needles, also called jersey needles, typically come in sizes 70/10 to 100/16. Use a smaller needle for finer knits and a larger needle for heavier fabrics.

If a knit has a significant amount of spandex or Lycra, consider using a stretch needle instead. Just like a jersey needle, stretch needles have a ballpoint intended for knit fabric, but the eye and scarf of the needle are specially designed to help when sewing elastic and also help avoid the skipped stitches, which are commonly associated with sewing stretch fabrics. Stretch needles typically come in two sizes: 75/11 and 90/14.

PRESSER FOOT PRESSURE AND EVEN FEED FOOT

The presser foot of a sewing machine holds the fabric against your feed dogs as you sew. This action is what feeds fabric through the sewing machine. The amount of pressure the presser foot delivers to the feed dogs directly affects how your fabric looks when removed from your sewing machine. If the pressure is set too high, the result will be stretched out fabric that is rippled in appearance. To avoid this, adjust your presser foot pressure. Typically a setting of 1 or lower is appropriate for knit fabrics.

The location of this dial or lever can vary from machine to machine. Refer to your machine manual to learn more about the presser foot pressure on your sewing machine.

An even feed foot or walking foot can also be helpful to gently and uniformly feed your fabric. An even feed foot has feed dogs that help to pull your fabric through your machine at a more even rate. This can be a helpful tool when working with finer, more delicate knits. When shopping for an even feed foot be sure to purchase one that is intended for your sewing machine. Like most machine accessories, walking feet are specific to the brand of sewing machine being used.

SEAMING

When working with wovens, the average seam consists of two parts. The first part is your construction stitch; this is typically a straight stitch. The second component to a seam is a finishing stitch. These are like a zigzag stitch or other overcast stitches that finish the raw edges of your fabric and keep your project from unraveling. When working with

Note: The seam guides on your sewing machine are only accurate when the needle is in the center position. When using stitches other than a straight stitch for construction, be sure to use a small ruler and painter's tape to mark a new seam guide suitable for the stitch you are using.

knit fabrics you can use one stitch to do the job of two. This is one of the many perks of working with knits! Here are some stitches that are ideal for the task of seaming knits.

It can be a helpful exercise to look at the inside of a few of your favorite knit garments. Look at the stitches being used to construct the garment. The first thing you might notice is the width of the stitches being used. The typical overlock stitch is 1/4" in width. This width provides strength as well as stretch and is what we want to mirror when sewing knits on a home sewing machine.

ZIG-ZAG STITCH

A zigzag stitch is a great way to seam knit fabrics. Its inherent stretch allows for the fabric to

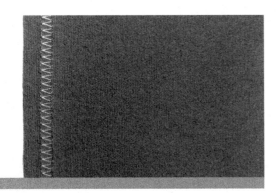

stretch and move without fear of popping a seam. On light to medium weight knits, try using a stitch length of 1.5 and a width of 5. This setting closely mimics the look and function of an overlock stitch. When sewing, remember to backstitch at the beginning and end of every seam to secure. To finish, trim the seam allowance close to stitching. This will closely emulate an overlock stitch and allow for maximum stretch and strength.

FAUX OVERLOCK STITCH

Most sewing machines will offer a variety of stretch stitches, many of which are intended to mimic the look of a serged edge. These stitches are aptly named

From left to right: a knit garment with a single fold hem, and a double fold hem on a woven garment.

overlock stitches. Check your sewing machine manual for the recommended stitch settings, though typically they tend to use a wide width and a short length. Keep in mind that many of these stitches will use a back-and-forth stitch path to create an elastic stitch. To avoid stretching when using this style of stitch merely support and gently guide fabric through the throat of the sewing machine. Resist the urge to stretch and sew! Backstitch to secure stitching and trim to neaten the seam allowance edges.

REINFORCED STRAIGHT STITCH

When working with thicker knits like ponte or heavy double knits, pressing the seam allowance open may be necessary. In these cases, a reinforced straight stitch can be used to create strong and flexible seams. A reinforced straight stitch is created by the needle moving forward and backward in a straight line, placing three parallel stitches side by side.

HEMMING

The biggest difference between hemming wovens versus knits, is that knits should be finished with a single fold hem. A double fold hem can create unnecessary bulk and cause the hem to roll toward the right side. When hemming knits at home, it is important to create a stitch that will stretch with your fabric. With these

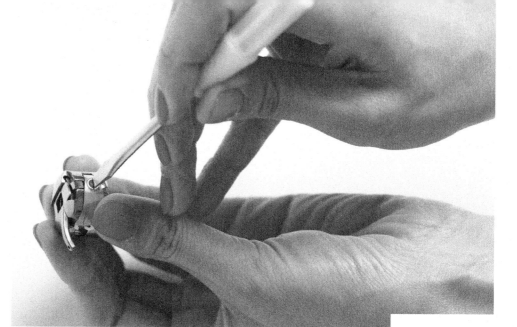

Use a small flat-head screw driver to loosen the tension of your bobbin case.

When planning your hem finish, it is important to consider the fit of your garment.

On the left an example of tunneling created by using a twin needle.
On the right a perfect finish after a small adjustment to the bobbin tension.

qualities in mind you have a few different options. In ready-to-wear, most knits are finished with a single fold hem and a machine called a coverstitch. A coverstitch machine produces a couple stitches: a chain stitch and a single or double-sided coverstitch. A chain stitch looks like a standard straight stitch from the right side but has a looped chain look on the wrong side; this is what gives the stitch its stretch. A single-sided coverstitch has two lines of parallel stitching on the right side, and on the reverse side it has the appearance of an overlock stitch. A double-sided coverstitch has the look of an overlock stitch on either side of the hem.

When planning your hem finish, it is important to consider the fit of your garment. The hem width will determine the amount of stretch the hem will need in order to get the garment on and off.

TWIN NEEDLE: FOR FITTED KNITS

A twin needle is your best bet if trying to imitate the look of a coverstitch. The stitch created when using a twin needle has the appearance of coverstitch from the right side, but on the wrong side, it looks like a zigzag stitch. This stitch has inherent stretch and is excellent for close-fitting knit garments. It is also highly beneficial to use when hemming jersey. The double stitching will

help the hem from rolling toward the right side when wearing.

A twin needle will fit into any standard sewing machine. It has a single shank that is easily inserted just like a typical needle. Check your sewing machine manual to learn about threading for your make and model of machine. The tension and length settings recommended for twin needle use can also vary depending on your machine.

Tunneling is a problem commonly associated with twin needles. This is when the space between the two stitches is raised, creating a tunnel. To avoid tunneling, knit stay tape can be used to stabilize the hem of your knit garments by offering additional support without adding bulk to your hem.

NARROW ZIGZAG: FOR GARMENTS WITH EASE

This can be an excellent option for wider hems that do not require huge amounts of stretch. At first glance this finish looks just like a straight stitch, but upon closer inspection you can see the small amount of width that gives the stitch just enough stretch. Set your machine up for a standard zigzag stitch. Adjust your width to be a very narrow 0.5 and your length to be just a bit longer than normal, approximately 3 (this may vary depending on how heavy or light your fabric is, so always test). You can also use a wider zigzag stitch to hem knitwear. The appearance of this can be very subtle if your thread is well-matched.

With these easy to follow techniques and tips, your next knitwear project will be a success.

There is no reason to fear knits.

REINFORCED STRAIGHT STITCH: FOR FIRM KNITS

A reinforced straight stitch can also be used to create the stretchable hem required for knits. Since this stitch creates a very bold stitching line, only use this technique when your thread matches perfectly or if you are using an intentionally contrasting thread color. The reinforced straight stitch is ideal for hemming stable knits that are firm with a fair amount of structure. This finish is not ideal for spongy knits, as it will produce an inconsistent finish. Avoid this method if you are working with a jersey knit that has a high tendency to roll toward the right side.

There is no reason to fear knits. With these easy to follow techniques and tips, your next knitwear project will be a success. So grab some ballpoint needles and that cut of knit fabric that has been hanging out in your stash for far too long! With a little know how and the correct tools you fall in love with sewing knits.

Haley Glenn is the Managing Editor for Seamwork. She is a professional sewing writer and teacher based in Portland, Oregon.

EMBROIDERED
Snow Flurry

*Festoon your skirts with garlands of embroidered
snowflakes, using just a few simple stitches.*

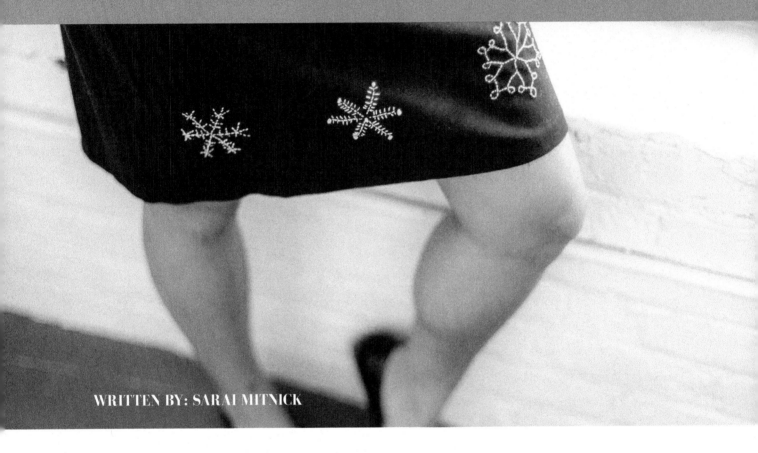

WRITTEN BY: SARAI MITNICK

These sweet star-like snowflakes were inspired by scientific illustrations found in an antique book. Rendered simply in white embroidery floss on a deep black or ink blue fabric, they're lovely wrapping around the hem of a skirt or dress. You could also sprinkle them over the entire garment, like a gentle snowfall.

Even if you've never embroidered a thing in your life, you'll find these snowflakes simple to complete. All you need are four basic stitches - a running stitch, back stitch, chain stitch, and French knot. These designs are so simple, you can use any of these stitches with our free embroidery pattern to create a wide variety of snowflakes. Download the pattern here: www.seamwork.com/go/embroidered-snowflakes

> **All you need are four basic stitches - a running stitch, back stitch, chain stitch, and French knot.**

Dress shown: Dahlia by Colette Patterns, sold separately.

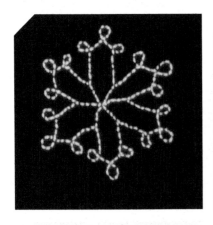

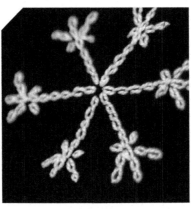

This snowflake uses the back stitch to create simple lines.

The chain stitch is used to create this design.

The back stitch and heavy French knots are combined in this motif.

THE BASICS OF EMBROIDERY

YOU'LL NEED:

- ◪ Free snowflake embroidery pattern
- ◪ Dressmaker's tracing paper
- ◪ Water soluble marking pencil
- ◪ Embroidery hoop
- ◪ Embroidery needle
- ◪ Embroidery floss, such as size 5 perle cotton

THE BASICS OF EMBROIDERY

Download the free pattern and use dressmaker's tracing paper to transfer the designs to your fabric. Once the design is transferred, use a water-soluble pencil to go over any portions of the design that are difficult to see. You can also draw additional design elements freehand at this point.

Position the snowflakes wherever you'd like on your garment. Place the embroidery hoop around each design and embroider one at a time, using a variety of stitches to vary the look of each motif. See the section below to learn each stitch.

For these designs, we used DMC perle cotton is size 5. This mercerized twisted cotton thread has a beautiful sheen and soft hand. It gives a beautiful dimension to these snowflakes.

For a similar but finer look, use perle cotton is size 3. This is another appropriate size for embroidery and will lend itself to intricate detail, although the result will be not quite as bold.

Learn the stitches below, then experiment with each of the snowflakes to create a series of different designs.

Mix and match the stitches with different motifs to create a huge variety of designs.

THE RUNNING STITCH

The running stitch is incredibly simple and easy to do. While it's shown here with large stitches, it can also be created with small stitches or fine thread. Parallel rows of running stitch can also be used to create thick lines and borders.

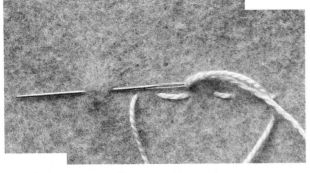

01 Run the needle in and out of the fabric to create a stitch.

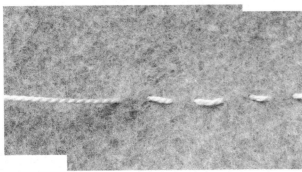

02 Create even spaces between stitches as you continue. The running stitch can be varied in many ways, by changing the length of the stitch and the spacing between the stitches.

THE BACK STITCH

The back stitch is a common stitch, used to create lines or outline blocks of color.
The back stitch is worked from right to left.

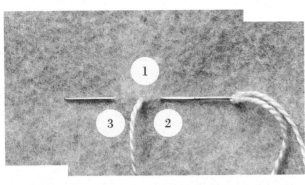

01 Bring the needle up through the fabric (1). Move the needle to the right, taking a small back stitch and insert into the fabric at (2), bring the point up in front of (1) at point (3). Point (1) should be halfway between points (2) and (3).

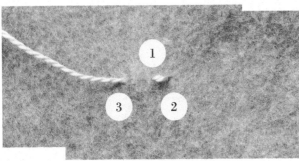

02 Pull the needle through.

Insert again at (1) and out again at point (4).

03

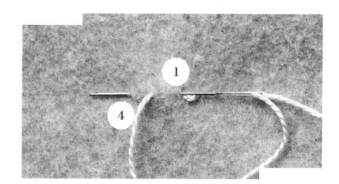

Pull the needle through. Repeat this process to continue.

04

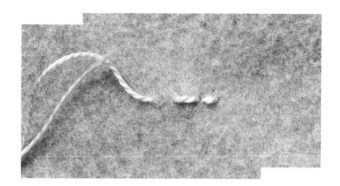

THE CHAIN STITCH

The chain stitch is a beautiful and simple way to create lines with texture and thickness. The stitch forms a series of interconnected loops that work well in both heavy thread with large stitches, and fine thread with small stitches.

Insert the needle at point (1) and back up at point (2). Loop the thread down to the left and under the tip of the needle. Pull the needle through, gently tugging the thread to form a loop. Insert the needle back in point (2) and repeat to form the next stitch in the chain.

01

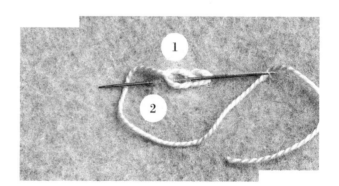

Experiment with thread weights to vary the look of your snowflakes.

THE FRENCH KNOT

The French knot can be used as an accent in a design, or it can be stitched in rows to form outlines. These knotted stitches may be placed around the edges of the snowflakes, in the center, or they may form an entire design.

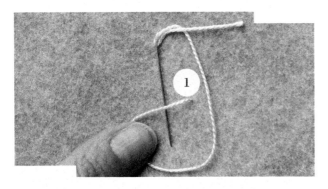

01 Bring the needle through the fabric at point (1). Holding the thread down with your thumb to the left of point (1), slide the tip of the needle under the taut thread.

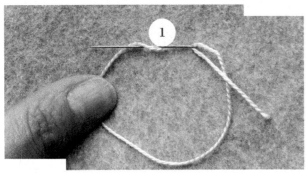

02 Rotate the needle in a clockwise motion, with the point of the needle on top of the thread.

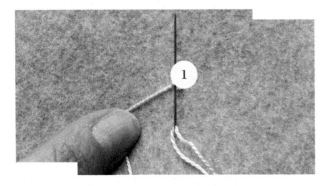

03 Rotate until the needle is pointing directly upward. There should be a single loop of thread around the needle.

Insert the tip of the needle right next to point (1), keeping the loop on the needle. Pull the needle and thread all the way to the back, creating a knot.

04

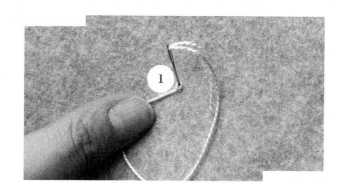

A finished French knot is small and subtle. To create larger, heavier knots, you may wrap the thread around the needle several times before pulling the needle all the way through.

05

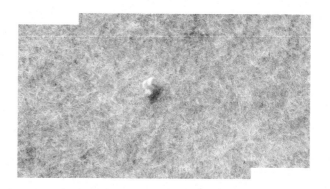

Get your free embroidery pattern here: www.seamwork.com/go/em-broidered-snowflakes

 Sarai Mitnick is the Editor-in-Chief of Seamwork Magazine and Founder of Colette. She often thinks and writes about the way sewing impacts our lives - through body image, identity, and social awareness.

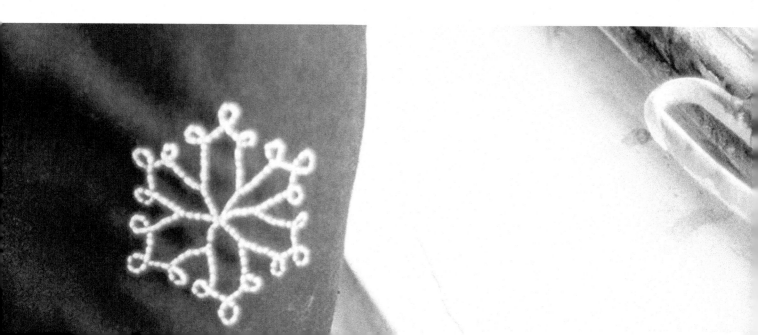

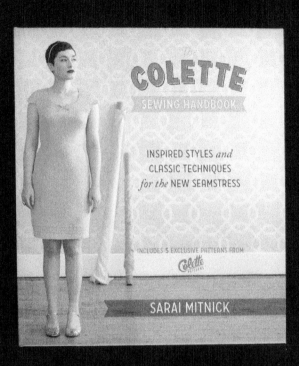

TEXTILES

Finding and making the perfect fabric.

The Art of Marbled Fabric

Good Silk Hunting

Farm to Fabric the story of Wool

THE ART OF
Marbled Fabric

*The centuries-old techniques
used to create marbled papers
can be used at home to make
gorgeous silks, cottons, and more.*

WRITTEN BY: SARAI MITNICK

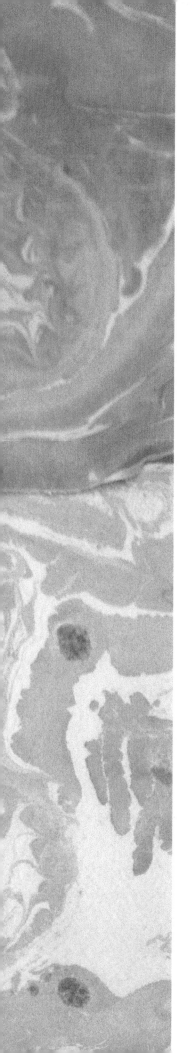

The Florence bralette with marble-dyed
cups and the Geneva panties in marble-
dyed stretch silk.

Many years ago, I was visiting Florence, Italy and stopped into a stationery shop. The tiny store was filled with creamy papers, handmade leather books, and beautiful fountain pens. On a table, I saw a small stack of notebooks with colorful marbled covers. Their swirling patterns were so intricate and dynamic, I couldn't help but imagine them on clothing.

Marbling is a technique used to create these surface designs that resemble the patterns found in stone. It's been used for many years to create book covers and end papers, but its history and application go far beyond that.

Marbling has been used to create decorative papers and books for centuries. These papers were marbled by textile artist Natalie Stopka.

The earliest known examples of marbling date back to Japan in the 12th century, where a technique known as *suminagashi*, meaning "floating ink" was used to create papers. Some scholars believe this art form was practiced even earlier in China, though no known examples exist. *Suminagashi* is still practiced in Japan today.

Similar methods also arose in central Asia in the 15th century. In Turkey, marbled papers were used to help prevent document forgery, since the designs were impossible to replicate exactly. This gave marbled papers a greater significance within the powerful Turkish empire, and the tradition remains strong in countries such as Iran and Turkey.

Finally, these methods spread from the middle east to Europe in the 17th century, where various countries each made their own adjustments and created signature patterns. This is the period in which marbled endpapers became popular in bookbinding, and you can still find these in use today.

But marbling is no longer limited to these traditional applications. Today, it's used to create artwork, fine papers, and fabric designs. Part of the beauty of marbling is that no two finished pieces are exactly alike, as the Turks discovered centuries ago. Textile artist Natalie Stopka, who creates marbled works and teaches workshops on large scale fabric marbling, says, "Marbling is a very expressive art. Each print is the culmination of a tiny performance in which the artist interacts with a fluid medium, revealing their temperament. Whether you are a fastidious craftsperson or relish experimentation, the marbling process will manifest your hand and aesthetic."

You'll need fabric, a frame, combs or other tools, paint, mixing tools, medium, and alum.

GETTING STARTED

Marbling at home requires just a few special tools and supplies. Get set up with the basics before beginning to experiment.

Despite the intricate results, the practice of marbling is simple at its core. Paints are floated on top of a gelatinous solution thick enough to allow them to remain on the surface. The craftsperson then creates patterns in the paint by raking through with simple utensils. Finally, a pretreated piece of cloth is lowered onto the surface, removed, rinsed, and set.

CHOOSING YOUR PROJECT

For the beginner, it's best to start with small pieces of fabric. As you will see, marbling large pieces requires a great deal of workspace and the construction of large frames, whereas small pieces can be marbled in kitchen tubs or pans. This makes marbling a perfect technique to try on lingerie pieces such as silk bras and panties, but you can also use it on pillows, kerchiefs, bias tape trims, or small insets or pieces in larger garments. For example, you could use marbling on the yoke of a shirt, the placket of a blouse, or anywhere else a small pattern piece is used.

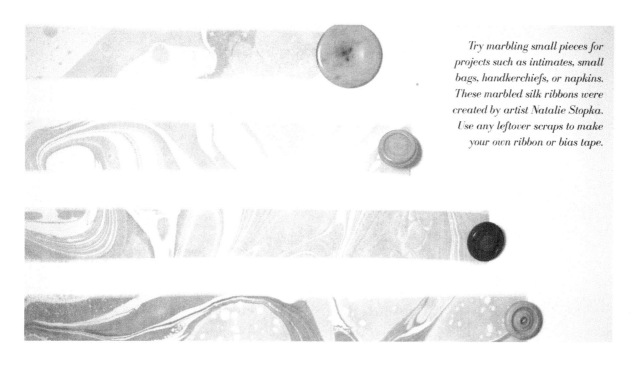

Try marbling small pieces for projects such as intimates, small bags, handkerchiefs, or napkins. These marbled silk ribbons were created by artist Natalie Stopka. Use any leftover scraps to make your own ribbon or bias tape.

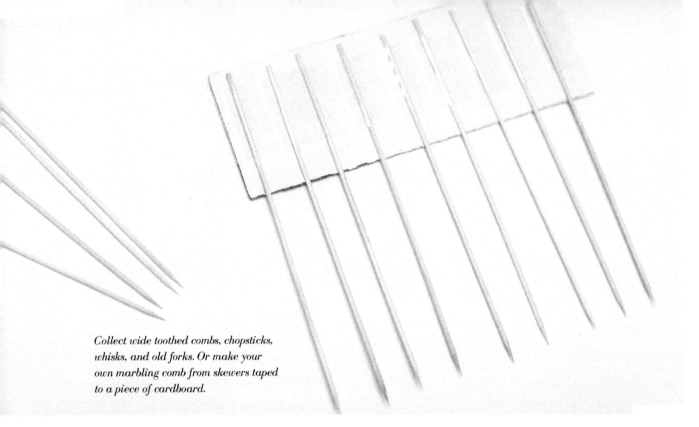

Collect wide toothed combs, chopsticks, whisks, and old forks. Or make your own marbling comb from skewers taped to a piece of cardboard.

THE FRAME

You will need a frame to hold the medium (also known as "size"), and it must be large enough to accommodate your fabric piece with at least an inch of room on all sides. For small pieces, you can use an inexpensive cake or lasagna pan from the grocery store, or a larger dish pan. This is what we will cover in this demonstration, since they are easy to find and perfect for beginner projects. Small frames are also easier to work with and provide more surface tension, so paints float more easily.

Once you've developed greater skills and want to branch out into larger projects, you can construct your own frame for marbling using 1 inch by 4 inch framing wood of any length you'd like. Create a large rectangle and use metal angle brackets at the corners to secure the shape. Finally, line the bottom and sides with clear plastic to hold the medium and paint. The plastic keeps the paint and medium from seeping out, without requiring you to build a bottom for your frame, which makes it heavier and harder to store.

Marbling pattern tools

In addition to the frame, you'll need tools to create the designs on the surface. The most common ready-made implements are wide-tooth combs, forks, or chopsticks. These are all easy to find and make sense to start with.

Many experienced marblers use combs specifically designed for marbling, and these extend almost to the edges of the frame, allowing you to create even designs. You can easily create your own marbling comb using toothpicks or skewers pushed through a piece of sturdy foam, or taped securely to a piece of cardboard. You could also force heavy pins through a piece of cardboard. Just make sure the tines of your comb are evenly spaced, and that the total length is at least 1 to 2 inches shorter than the frame.

Paint mixing and dropping tools

You will also need a few simple tools for mixing up the paint, thinning it as needed, and dropping it onto the surface of the medium. Small plastic paint mixing cups with lids work fine and allow you to see the colors easily. You can also use disposable cups if you like, or other small cups dedicated to paint.

For dropping the paint, I prefer an eyedropper. Eyedroppers allow you to release small quantities of paint at a time into the medium, which prevents it from sinking to the bottom. Pouring in too much paint at once, or from too great a height, will keep it from floating on the surface where it comes into contact with the fabric.

Medium

Many sorts of medium (also known as "size") are available for home marbling. The job of this substance is to provide a thick, gelatinous, but still aqueous surface for the paint to sit on. Some home marblers have even used watered down wallpaper paste! The amount of medium you need will depend on the size of your frame. You want enough medium to fill the frame 1 to 2 inches deep. You can easily determine how much you need by pouring water into the frame until it reaches this depth, then measuring the water as you pour it out.

The most popular option for medium is carrageen, a non-toxic thickener made from seaweed. There are two types of carrageen: blender carrageen and heated carrageen. Both should be prepared 12-24 hours before use, to allow time to thicken. Blender carrageen is easier to

Blender carrageen is used to make small quantities

make in small batches, whereas heated carrageen is useful for large quantities.

To prepare blender carrageen, place water in your blender and begin blending. With the blender running, add 1 teaspoon of carrageen for every 2 cups of water. Make the medium in batches if necessary. Blend for about 30 seconds. You should have a thick, uniform consistency. Place the substance in the refrigerator overnight, and remove and allow to come to room temperature before using.

For heated carrageen, use a gallon of water. Pour 4 cups of this into a pot and heat to a simmer. Pour into a bucket and add 5 tablespoons of the carrageen powder along with a little more water to cool the mixture

enough to immerse your hands. Mix thoroughly with a stick, or use your hands to break up any clumps. Stir in the rest of the water, and refrigerate overnight. Again, allow the mixture to come to room temperature before using.

Methocel is another option for medium. The advantage of methocel is that it can be mixed just 30 minutes before you begin, so there is no need to let it sit overnight. To create this medium, place a gallon of warm water in a bucket, then add 1 Tablespoon of ammonia. Finally, stir in 1/4 cup of methocel, a little at a time, stirring constantly with a large stick or a whisk. Once dissolved, let the medium sit for 30 minutes.

You can mix a variety of colors from red, yellow, blue, and white.

Fabric

Many types of fabric can be used for marbling, but for best results, use a fabric with a smooth texture and fine weave. Heavily textured fabrics will not show the patterns quite as well.

Experiment with different fibers to see what works best with your paints. Silk is always a great choice because it absorbs color well and often has a luxuriously smooth, fine texture. For the Florence bralette and Geneva panties, we used a silk/spandex charmeuse, also known as stretch silk. Linen, cotton, and other fibers can also be used, as well as synthetics. This is a great excuse to use up the scraps you've been saving.

Alum

Alum will help the colors from the paint set on the fabric, preventing them from bleeding out later. Begin by pre-washing the fabric with detergent, preferably an industrial textile detergent such as synthrapol. This will remove any manufacturing chemicals, dirt, or oil before you begin. It's best to do this 12-24 hours before you marble, so do it at the same time that you create the medium.

Dissolve alum in hot water, at a ratio of 3 tablespoons per quart. Allow the mixture to come back to room temperature. Swirl the fabric in the mixture, allowing it to become saturated, and then remove it quickly. Squeeze to remove excess water and hang dry. Don't apply heat after treating with alum until you rinse it out later, as this can damage the fabric. Line drying helps prevent wrinkles from forming.

Paint

Acrylic paints or airbrushing ink are the most common choices for fabric marbling. Acrylic paints can be purchased from any art supply or craft store, but it's best to be consistent with the brand so that they mix well and have similar viscosity.

Airbrush inks create gorgeous colors that work well on many fabrics, though they sometimes must be mail ordered. For this demonstration, I used Jacquard airbrush inks.

You do not need many colors to begin, since the paints can be mixed. Red, yellow, and blue will allow you to create a large range of colors from these primary hues. You may also wish to purchase black and white. These few colors should get you started.

Depending on the type of paint you use, you may need to dilute them a bit to allow them to float on the surface. Test a bit first on your medium before you begin, gently placing one drop of paint on the surface. If it seems to sink to the bottom, start thinning the paint. In a small mixing cup, add a couple drops of water or dispersant to the paint and mix. Try adding it to the medium again. Repeat until the paint floats easily on the surface, but still remains in a roughly circular shape.

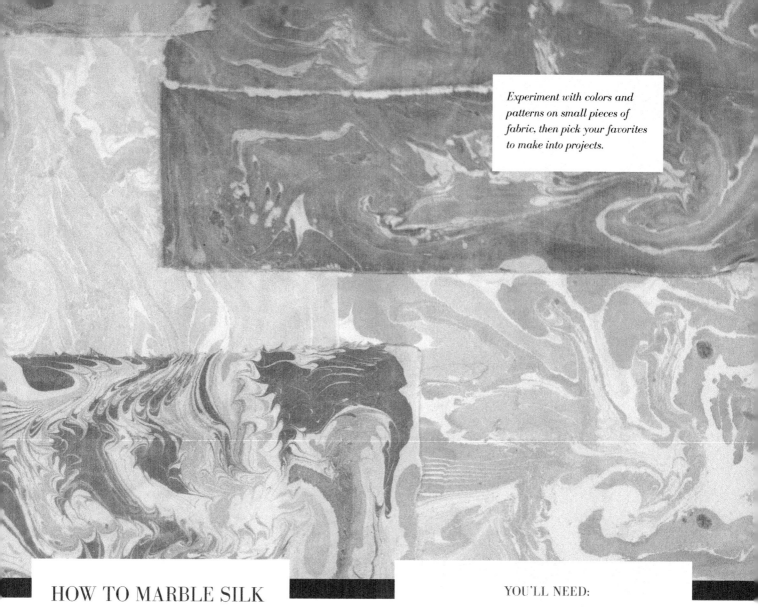

HOW TO MARBLE SILK

Now that you have all the supplies and basics down, let's walk through a single marbling project together. We'll dye pieces of silk charmeuse that can be used for creating the Florence bralette cups and Geneva panties. Want to keep it simple? Dharma Trading Company sells marbling starter sets that contain many of these supplies. All you need to add are the tools: frame, mixing cups, comb, and eyedroppers.

YOU'LL NEED:

- [ ] Three pieces of silk (we used 11" x 17" pieces for a size small)
- [ ] Alum
- [ ] One plastic bucket for pre-treating fabric
- [ ] One large rectangular dishpan to use as a frame (we used 12" x 18")
- [ ] Carrageen (blender type)
- [ ] Jacquard airbrush inks
- [ ] Eyedroppers
- [ ] Small paint mixing cups
- [ ] A large comb, chopsticks, and/or homemade marbling comb (see Marbling pattern tools)

01 12 to 24 hours before marbling, prepare the medium using the blender method (see instructions Medium). The mixture will be foamy at first. Rest in the refrigerator overnight to allow air to come to the surface.

02 At the same time, pre-wash and pre-treat your fabric using alum (see instructions under Alum). Allow to dry while your medium rests.

03 About one hour before marbling, remove the medium from the refrigerator and allow to come to room temperature.

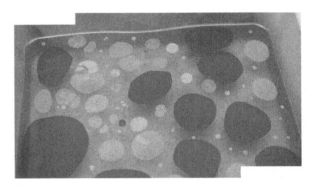

04 Mix your paint colors. Add a few drops to the medium and check to see if they float, yet remain consistent in the medium. If not, adjust the paint by thinning it with water or dispersant. Continue adding paint, drop by drop.

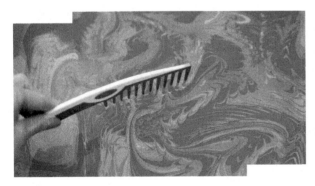

05 Using tools such as a wide comb, fork, or chopsticks, drag lightly through the surface to create patterns. Drag in straight lines, swirls, or any other pattern you'd like.

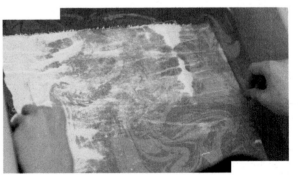

06 Lay your piece of fabric on the surface, allowing the middle of the fabric to contact the solution first, then lower the edges. It can be helpful to have a friend help, but this isn't strictly necessary for small pieces.

07 Lift the fabric out of the water, gently peeling it away from the surface. The remaining paint can be scooped from the surface of the medium with strips of newspaper, allowing you to marble the next piece.

08 Rinse the fabric in cool water, being careful not to wring or twist the fabric. Line dry, or lay flat. Once dry, iron the fabric to heat set the design and prevent future bleeding.

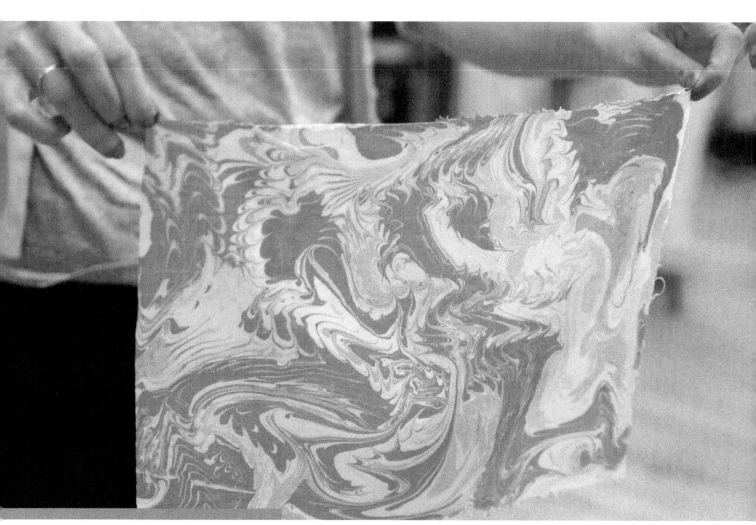

Your fabric can now be used to create beautiful garments, crafts, or home decor. Try marbling silk and using it to create the Geneva panties from this month's issue!

Sarai Mitnick is the Editor-in-Chief of Seamwork Magazine and Founder of Colette. She often thinks and writes about the way sewing impacts our lives - through body image, identity, and social awareness.

GOOD SILK
HUNTING

WRITTEN BY:
HEATHER LEWENZA

An investigation into where our fabric comes from.

> Where does our fabric come from? Who decides what will be sold in stores? And why can't I find any freaking chambray?

Sewing my own clothes has always made me feel a little euphoric. I'll never stop being amazed when random idea fragments evolve into making actual physical garments with my own two hands. Unfortunately, that sewing euphoria is often tempered by reality. I am talking about those heart-breaking trips to the fabric store where the materials you've been fantasizing about can't be found anywhere—polyester everywhere and not a drop of silk to drink.

I design sewing patterns, and as my own sewing practice has shifted from hobby to career, my fabric consumption has increased tenfold. I'm always hunting for the right material for designs I'm working on and am continually surprised by how difficult it is to find the good stuff: silk crepe and noil, Breton striped knits, exuberantly printed rayon challis, non-acrylic sweater knits, non-pilling ponte, and stretch denim that actually holds its shape. I've watched sewing explode in popularity over the last few years, and I'm frequently stumped by how slowly the market has evolved to serve the new renaissance of makers who are

approaching sewing from more of a ready-to-wear point of view than ever before.

On my own personal fabric quest, I've stopped shopping at the discount stores loaded with polar fleece and polyester chiffon and ventured into the wholesale warehouses of Montreal, Canada's rag trade district. Cavernous, messy, chaotic places crammed with pallets and rolls upon rolls of fabric, the district's wholesalers sell primarily to designers and fabric stores. The more I started to talk to the warehouse owners, the more curious I became about the fabric industry itself. Where does our fabric come from? Who decides what will be sold in stores? And why can't I find any freaking chambray?

Christopher Higgins owns Globe-tex, a crammed-to-the-gills warehouse

Christopher Higgins, owner of the Globetex fabric warehouse in Montreal.

in Montreal that's open to the public. With twenty years of experience, he has seen the fabric industry change dramatically over the course of his career: "Free trade and globalization have totally changed the market. It's caused a lot of pain for a lot of people and it's decimated the manufacturing sector altogether. We've lost our mills, the technical experts who operate the mills, the chemists who understand dyeing, the engineers who know how to design the textiles."

Since most fabric and clothing manufacturing moved overseas in the past two decades and dropped dramatically in price, home sewing dropped off as well. Sewing used to be the way to build a wardrobe without spending a lot of money, but it has now become more affordable to buy than make. Why sew a dress when you can snag one for $15 at the mall?

An overwhelming amount of cheaply made clothing is available everywhere, but ironically, it's encouraging people to return to sewing once again. We miss quality. We want to feel creative and connected, and to avoid wearing clothing made in dangerous and exploitative sweatshops. We are a movement, and the fabric industry is catching up to us, slowly but surely.

It's evident in the emergence of many new online fabric stores. Blackbird Fabrics is relatively fresh on the scene. However, its owner, Caroline Somos, has years of experience working in the fabric industry, primarily at Télio, one of Canada's largest fabric wholesalers. Caroline explains, "There is this new wave of DIY right now where people want to take it a step further. We're

Caroline Somos owns Blackbird Fabrics, an online retailer specializing in dressmaking supplies.

> **"**
>
> *We are a movement,*
> *and the fabric industry*
> *is catching up to us,*
> *slowly but surely.*

not sewing clothes because we have to, we're doing it because we want to." She understands all too well the frustration of trying to source desirable fabrics: "What we need is more quality fashion textiles readily available to the masses!"

We're at an interesting point in the sewing renaissance; while brick and mortar shops close left and right, a market-savvy entrepreneur can do well online by understanding the needs of a fabric-hungry market. You may know Sunni Standing, who writes the long-running sewing blog A Fashionable Stitch. She recently closed her physical shop in Salt Lake City, Utah in order to focus on teaching sewing workshops and maintaining her thriving, online haberdashery. "Online, of course, caters to a much larger audience and so by virtue, you automatically have a much larger customer base...I see the younger generation up and coming in the online community and they are much more confident in making purchases online when it comes to fabric, especially when you show them how it looks in a garment."

Regardless of whether or not a fabric store exists online or on Main Street, all fabric merchandise is channeled through a secretive, competitive network of jobbers and wholesalers. By understanding their client base and market, a savvy fabric store may be able to get their hands on the "good stuff," provided they can find it from one of the following suppliers:

Jobbers are key players in the fabric industry. They buy lots of off-cuts, leftovers, and factory seconds in limited quantities from mills, desig-

ners, and clothing manufacturers, and they redistribute the fabric to retailers and wholesalers. "With jobbers you tend to find a mish-mash. There are definitely deals to be had, and gorgeous fabrics from time to time. But it takes more digging and there is usually zero chance of coming back and finding more of something you like," says Caroline. According to Christopher Higgins of Globetex, approximately 80% of fabric in stores is recycled from ready-to-wear, largely through the efforts of the jobber industry.

Wholesalers can function as jobbers, but they are more reliable and valuable for the regular lines and merchandise they carry. Fabric retailers and designers can depend on them to have consistent stock from month to month. One you may have heard of is Robert Kaufman Fabrics, a reputable American company, which sells fabric across the spectrum; behemoths like Fabric.com and smaller shops like Grey's Fabric and Notions carry their goods. Caroline explains, "Wholesalers often have a showroom and a 'line' of fabric that is somewhat cohesive. They also have the advantage of being able to develop custom colors or prints, and restock items if they are in high demand."

Mills sometimes provide fabric directly to retailers, and a few businesses actually have custom fabric made exclusively. Girl Charlee Fabrics is a popular online store known primarily for their knits. The owner, Heather Peterson, told me, "We make our own collection that is produced on fabrics that are both knitted and printed here in Los Angeles, California. We started designing and printing our own fabrics as I love a certain aesthetic and could never find it in the marketplace." While this

kind of direct relationship between manufacturer and retailer is not the norm, it's sure to become more commonplace as more and more creative online businesses emerge.

Even with a growing range of retailers selling fabric, why is it still so hard for me to find a variety of modern, printed silks and interesting wools? "These are fabrics that are hard for everyone to find! They are hard for me to get as a retailer. All the fabrics you want are what we all want. The sewing trend did go 'soft' and so with it, many of these lovely fabrics can no longer be sourced. But as sewing keeps on trending, we can all hope to see the return of many of these fabrics, and hopefully more," explains Sunni.

Part of the problem is the way we, as a society, perceive cost. In a globalized world, we are used to our merchandise being cheap and plentiful. The reality is, genuine quality doesn't come cheap. My wholesaler, Christopher, doesn't carry as much high-end stock as he would like. "I have a hard time moving more expensive fabric. I can get silk in and wholesale it for $10-12 a yard, but my clients will complain that it's too expensive and it just sits in my warehouse. Unfortunately I can't keep buying fabric that people don't want to pay for, even if I personally love it."

Sunni knows firsthand about the problems that come with stocking high-end fabrics: "The majority of my brick and mortar customer base were extremely budget conscious. I would see many of my customers frequent Joann and Hancock chain stores, yet only come to my store for something special or wedding dress fabric. It could be very frustrating because even though I had a shop filled to the brim with beautiful cloth, we never seemed to have exactly what people wanted - unless it was on sale! And I don't say this to offend, I say it because it's true! It was incredibly frustrating day in and day out to see this happening."

Many of us are used to shopping at big-box fabric stores with their frequent bargain basement sales. They may have some regular lines sourced through wholesalers, but almost all of their stock is purchased

Tips on
SOURCING FABRIC

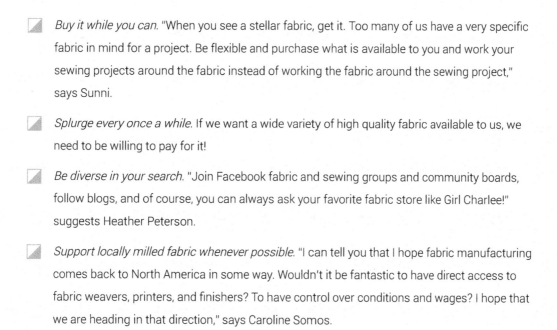

▨ *Buy it while you can.* "When you see a stellar fabric, get it. Too many of us have a very specific fabric in mind for a project. Be flexible and purchase what is available to you and work your sewing projects around the fabric instead of working the fabric around the sewing project," says Sunni.

▨ *Splurge every once a while.* If we want a wide variety of high quality fabric available to us, we need to be willing to pay for it!

▨ *Be diverse in your search.* "Join Facebook fabric and sewing groups and community boards, follow blogs, and of course, you can always ask your favorite fabric store like Girl Charlee!" suggests Heather Peterson.

▨ *Support locally milled fabric whenever possible.* "I can tell you that I hope fabric manufacturing comes back to North America in some way. Wouldn't it be fantastic to have direct access to fabric weavers, printers, and finishers? To have control over conditions and wages? I hope that we are heading in that direction," says Caroline Somos.

overseas by the shipping container, often in mixed lots for twenty-five cents a yard. Under those conditions, it's no wonder why it's difficult to find a gorgeous wool crepe or silk charmeuse at a chain store. It's all the more important to support independent businesses who genuinely love fabric and are more thoughtful and conscious about the wants and needs of their customers.

As the sewing renaissance picks up speed, we can expect to see fabric stores and manufacturers emerging to cater to this vibrant and diverse market. As our market share grows, so too do our options. Custom fabric printing services from companies like Spoonflower are exciting developments. Additionally, modern and forward-thinking quilting fabric companies like Cotton+Steel are starting to expand their range with new fabric options like my beloved rayon challis and voile. The future is bright for makers, and hopefully with

more of a fashion-savvy demand for fabric, we will expand the options available to us. Even better, perhaps a focus on quality, transparency, and accountability will help revitalize our local fabric-manufacturing sector, which used to be such a strong part of our economy. A girl can dream.

Heather Lewenza is the designer and blogger behind Closet Case Files. Visit her blog and purchase her patterns at closetcasefiles.com.

Farm to Fabric

THE STORY OF WOOL

WRITTEN BY: DEVON IOTT

A visit to a Tennessee farm reveals the miraculous processes that turn fleece to fabric.

❝*I*t's mostly Romneys up on that hill, but you can see a few Cotswolds mixed in. Over there are the Shetlands."

Kim Caulfield flicks a hand toward a nearby pasture as I pick my way after her across the muddy ground. Her sweatshirt, emblazoned with the image of a sheep, says, "To baa or not to baa." She is wearing a headband, which she knit herself, from yarn she spun and dyed herself, from sheep she raised herself. Kim walks with solid purpose, cutting a deliberate path across the soggy yard. Around us stand several large, fluffy Newfoundland dogs, and I have the odd sensation that I'm amongst a herd of friendly polar bears.

❝

She is wearing a headband that she knit herself, from yarn she spun and dyed herself, from sheep she raised herself.

I glance up amid careful puddle dodging and see the Shetland sheep bunched together in their paddock. They are small and nimble with large, glassy eyes, and they skitter away nervously as we pass. A few hop, and one is unable to suppress an alarmed bleat.

Kim looks at me and grins. Kim and her mother, Jane Caulfield, raise sheep on Far Out Farm in Delina, Tennessee, a one-stop-sign town nestled in the rolling hills about an hour south of Nashville. What started as a hobby twenty-five years ago has become a full-time business, with a flock of over a hundred sheep.

When I ask them how they got into it, they both laugh and point a finger at the other.

"It's her fault; she signed me up for weaving lessons," Kim explains.

"It's her fault, she really liked them," Jane replies.

ANCIENT WOOL

One of Kim's most prized possessions is a glass distaff dated to around the early second century. She gets it out of a case to show me. A distaff is a tool that twists wool fibers into yarn — the spinning wheel wasn't invented until around the year 1200. This one is a fragile rod about eight inches long made from beautifully whorled sea green glass. Both ends curve into a loop, creating eyes through which the wool fibers are passed. Kim hands it to me and I hold it, enthralled and terrified. It is impossibly fragile, unbelievably still in one piece. In places it is smooth with wear.

Kim jabs a finger at it. "Some woman spun yarn with this two thousand years ago," she says.

For thousands of years, the story of wool has been entwined with that of humanity's. People began to domesticate sheep nearly 10,000 years ago after realizing that they could provide both food and clothing. The herd animals could easily move with nomadic tribes, and their resiliency and ability to eat woody plants meant they could survive in conditions many other animals could not.

As societies evolved and cultures flourished, millennia of selective breeding created many varieties of sheep with differing characteristics. The Romans were expert shepherds, and as they conquered Europe, their flocks followed. Wool became a highly sought after and highly protected commodity. Spain, where the fine-wool Merino sheep originate, imposed the death penalty on the export of sheep until 1786. England discouraged a wool industry in the

In New Zealand, sheep outnumber people five- to-one.

American colonies, eventually making it illegal to raise and trade wool there. Like the Boston Tea Party, wool production became one of the many contested issues that led to the American Revolution.

In the following years, the wool industry grew with the onset of the Industrial Revolution, rising to meet the demands of an exploding population with ever increasing purchasing power. Wool began its steady decline following the invention of synthetic fibers in the mid-twentieth century. By the end of the 1990s, the US wool industry had collapsed to half its size. Unable to compete

with cheaper overseas production and the emergence of competing wool markets, many sheep farming operations were shuttered. Today, the industry is dominated by Australia, China, and New Zealand, where sheep outnumber citizens five to one.

SEASONAL SHEARING

Sheep shearing at Far Out Farm takes place in February; in cooler areas of the country, it generally takes place between March and June. Shearers, many of whom travel for work, are hired in for the job. Even on the large industrialized sheep ranches where herds may number in the

tens of thousands, there is still no way to safely remove a fleece from a sheep except by hand, one at a time. In-demand shearers sometimes work half the year in the northern hemisphere and the other half in the southern.

One might expect the shearing to take place in the summer when it's the hottest, but it is actually timed so that the sheep have grown a bit of fleece back by summer. Because of wool's insulating properties, sheep with an inch of fleece are actually cooler than sheep with no fleece. Sheep are unable to sweat; they pant like dogs when their body tempera-

ture gets too high, so overheating must be avoided.

The ups and downs of a sheep's year are recorded in every strand of their wool. If a sheep is sick or stressed, that point in the fleece is weakened and more prone to breakage. Intense heat can produce yellowed wool. Just like human hair, fleece is synthesized protein, so a well-fed, calm sheep will produce the best quality wool. Far Out Farm's sheep are raised on a diet of grass and hay with a custom-mixed mineral supplement. Kim and Jane avoid the use of fertilizer by carefully rotating the grass varieties they plant in each pasture.

QUALITY FLEECE

For very, very high quality wool, like the wool used for Italian designer suits, some farms jacket their sheep, a practice that dates back to the ancient Romans. The animals actually wear little sheep-sized jackets to protect their fleeces from the

> **"**
>
> *If there's one thing about fiber people, it's that we always want more fiber.*

elements. As the fleece grows, the jackets are swapped out for successively larger ones. The jacket keeps the fleece snowy white and protects against environmental undesirables like dead plants and bugs. Jacketed sheep are primarily found in Australia and New Zealand, and buyers fly in from around the world to source and purchase these fleeces.

So what makes a fleece better or worse? Softer or scratchier? It mostly comes down to two factors: fiber diameter and fiber length. When wool fabric is placed against the body, the scratchiness is actually created by all the ends of the wool fibers. If the fiber is thin enough, it will bend away when it touches the skin. If it is thick, it remains rigid, registering as a tiny poke. Long fibers mean there are fewer ends to poke the skin; shorter fibers mean more pokes. So the thicker and shorter the fibers in a particular variety of wool, the itchier.

Fine wool, like Merino, is the softest wool to wear. Its fibers have a diameter of under about twenty-five microns (a micron is one-millionth of a meter). At the other end of the spectrum, coarse wool fibers have a diameter of thirty-eight microns or more. This wool is too uncomfortable for clothing and is used for things like carpets and stuffing.

FIBER PEOPLE

Kim and Jane take me up to the attic of their processing building to look at some fiber. On the way, they proudly show me an elevator that they made, which I wholeheartedly

agree is quite impressive. A spinning enthusiast, Kim not only processes her own fiber, but she also buys it from others. She pulls out a tuft of purchased Merino wool and a tuft of her own Romney wool. The Merino is glossy, white, and tightly coiled. The Romney, while still soft, is a bit coarser.

The attic is littered with garbage bags of different fibers like silk, wool, bamboo, and angora. Kim mutters something dreamily about bison fiber, which, allegedly, is very soft.

"If there's one thing about fiber people," she says, nudging a dusty bag with her foot. "It's that we always want more fiber."

There are only a few woolen mills left in the United States, Pendleton perhaps being the best well known. Like sheep farmers, woolen mills simply couldn't compete with cheaper overseas services. However, as with other areas of agriculture, there has recently been a burgeoning new interest in the smaller scale, and a few mills are bravely popping up here and there. One such mill is Northern Woolen Mills in Fosston, Minne-

sota, where new owner Stephanie Anderson learned how to operate the equipment via YouTube videos.

These small mills come as great relief to small wool producers, who usually have to ship their raw wool very far to be processed. This is one of the factors that led Kim and Jane to hire an engineer to custom build a mill. It is the same equipment that a large, industrial-sized operation would use. Kim processes their own wool and also offers her services for hire. Her skills are in such high demand that she jokingly tells me to keep quiet about them, because she already has so much regional business that she can't keep up.

WASHING THE FLEECE

The whole process starts with a fleece, which is the wool from one sheep shorn in a single piece. One average-sized fleece could make about two adult sweaters. First, the unusable parts are removed. These are usually the skirtings, dirty, short-fibered portions, which are around the legs and underbelly of the animal. Kim and Jane stuff the skirtings into burlap bags and use them like sandbags to control erosion around the farm. The wool felts inside the bag and the burlap

rots away, leaving something behind that looks disconcertingly like a giant hairball.

Next, the wool must be washed. Raw wool is also called greasy wool, because it is soaked with lanolin. Even just touching it leaves a residue on your hands.

The naturally occurring lanolin helps protect the sheep and keep water out; however, it has a rather pungent smell and isn't desirable in the finished yarn. Not everyone in history agrees on this, though. The well-known Irish fisherman sweaters used to be made with greasy wool. The combination of the lanolin and the minor felting that happened with the ocean damp created a garment that was practically waterproof, if rather stinky.

The most important reason to wash wool is to prevent it from felting. Have you ever accidentally shrunk a sweater? That's felting. Wool fibers are covered with little shingles that stick out like barbs — imagine the close-up diagrams shown on shampoo commercials. Sheep's hair grows with barbs all in one direction, so they are able to flex and move over one another. When the wool is cut and made into fabric, however,

the fibers are rearranged and the barbs are all unaligned. If the fibers are agitated, the barbs lock together, irreversibly pulling the fibers close to each other.

MEET THE MACHINERY

Kim soaks her batches of wool in cool, soapy water; avoids heat and agitation; and then hangs it in bags to dry. After a few rounds of this, the wool is ready to go, sometimes weighing up to forty percent less after the removal of the lanolin and dirt.

The first machine the wool goes through is the picker. The fiber is loaded onto a conveyor belt, which sends it into a large spinning drum covered with spikes. This initial process starts to comb and separate the fibers and removes any large debris. The machine then shoots the fibers out into a little walled space with a door, essentially a closet built out in the center of the room.

During my visit, Kim has a batch in progress and starts running a little bit of it through so I can watch. The machine rumbles and spins, and the fleece disappears inside. Kim goes around to the back and opens the little door, grinning gleefully as wool fibers fly through the air and settle in fluffy drifts on the floor inside.

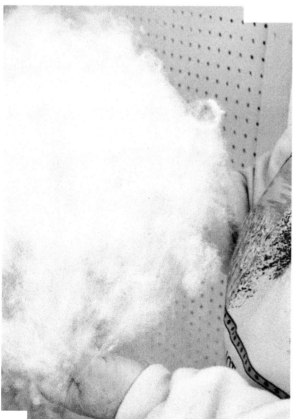

Wool is turned into roving, which can be spun into yarn.

She scoops up armfuls of wool and heads toward the next machine, the carder. This one looks rather like a medieval torture device that someone decided to repaint Kelly green. Drum upon drum, all different diameters, turning at different speeds, and covered with differently spaced spikes, is stacked in the center. The machine is contained in a large metal cage, not unlike a ferocious carnivorous beast, and Kim and Jane are sure to give me a small safety talk before they turn it on.

The drifts of wool are sent down a conveyer belt into the mouth of the machine, where spinning teeth grab and send them flying around the drums. As the wool goes through, spending more time on one drum, less time on another, it gets progressively cleaner and looks smoother. The whole point of carding is to comb the fibers so that they are

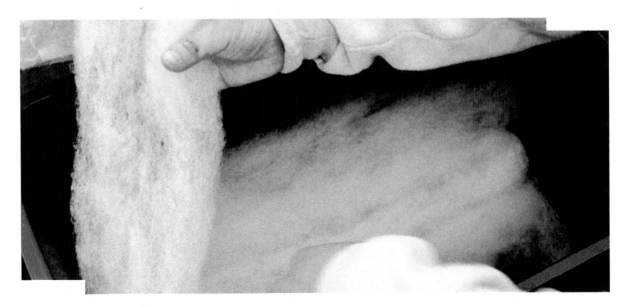

straight, elongated, and running in the same direction.

After the wool has completed its harrowing journey through the spikes, it comes out the other end in a smooth, round rope. This is called roving, and the wool is now ready to be spun into yarn.

It is not hyperbole to say that watching this transformation felt a little bit miraculous. Mere minutes before, the wool still looked pretty sheep-like; after minimal effort and only a few touches of human hands, it transformed into almost yarn. Carding machines are true feats of engineering, and it was one of those moments, like looking at the engine of a car or the wing of an airplane, when I suddenly feel deep gratitude for someone else's genius.

MAKING YARN

In a factory setting, the roving would then be spun into yarns of a small diameter, a size we'd think of as thread. There are two main categories of processing wool into yarns for fabric production: woolens and worsteds. Woolens are usually shorter, coarser fibers and spend less time being carded. They are made into fabrics like tweed. Worsteds go through extra steps in the carding process, resulting in softer and more comfortable fabrics.

Once the yarn is spun, a variety of treatments may be applied to it before it is woven or knit into fabric. There are several different chemical processes that can be applied to reduce or prevent felting, such as a chlorine wash to remove the fiber barbs or a resin that coats and smooths the fibers. Wool takes on dye very well, as its naturally porous composition eagerly soaks up and holds the color.

As a fabric, wool has a variety of properties that make it as attractive a material today as it was a thousand years ago. Molecularly, wool fibers are tiny coils, which look like little springs. This makes them highly elastic and allows them to bounce back into shape even after lots of stretching. The coil structure also creates lots of space to trap air and moisture. This is what makes wool warm, but not overly so. Wool is also hydroscopic, meaning it can absorb up to thirty percent of its own weight in water without feeling damp. It's one of the only fabrics that will still keep you warm when wet, and its naturally high moisture and nitrogen content means that it is extremely flame-resistant. Not too bad for a prehistoric fabric!

SUSTAINABLE WOOL

As the garment industry tries harder to sell more, concerns about the impact on our resources and our environment are being raised. Fast fashion means that clothes are disposable; these cheaply made, polyester garments are finding their way into landfills quicker than ever, where they take as long to decompose as a plastic bag.

Wool offers an attractive alternative. As a natural protein, it decomposes quickly and easily. Sheep require few resources to raise and can eat just about anything, making their environmental impact minimal. In fact, farmers are now using sheep in place of herbicides and insecticides.

They can be strategically grazed to control invasions of non-native plant species, being much cheaper—not to mention less toxic—than chemical weed killers. A recent study also found that grazing sheep in a wheat field post-harvest could significantly reduce the presence of insect pests in next year's crop.

A RECIPROCAL RELATIONSHIP

After the tour of their farm, Kim and Jane kindly take me out to lunch in Delina. The town café is also the town general store, and everyone inside knows each other like we're in a 1950s television show. An ancient, black, pot-bellied stove hunkers down on the creaking floorboards, and burgers sizzle on a griddle. On Kim's recommendation I order the fried green beans, which are crispy little bites of divinity. We all leave with hand pies to go, homemade and dropped off daily by a woman down the street.

On the drive back to the farm, Kim talks about her meticulous control over each year's breeding process, and how she selects which ewe to breed to which ram. The lambs with the most desirable characteristics are kept to integrate into the flock's

gene pool. Others are sold, or, as Kim puts it, "go to the freezer," discussing with a farmer's bluntness the process of birth, life, and death from which we're now all so removed.

Before I leave, we decide to take one last walk down to the Shetlands to see if Kim can coax one up close. Jane and I stay back to chat, and once again I'm surrounded by the Newfoundlands, who dwarf the Shetlands by nearly double.

A voice rings out, clear and strong, and I look to the distance to see Kim sitting on the ground in front of a sheep. I realize that she is singing. Her voice is trained, controlled, and clear as a bell, and remarkably incongruous with the raw damp of the farm. Her operatic vibrato lilts back to us in pieces, blown here and there by the breeze, the notes deliberate and solid.

A sheep takes a step toward Kim, seemingly entranced, and doesn't notice as she slowly reaches up and puts her arm around it. She continues to sing and it relaxes against her, glassy eyes going distant as she scratches it under the chin.

As we wait for Kim to work her magic, Jane apologizes that it's winter and I couldn't see the farm

when it was prettier, as if she wishes she could alter the changing of the seasons just for my visit.

I look around. The dormant fields are tapestries of gold, sienna, and moss, and the skies above them are brilliant blue. Sheep lounge in the sun under the silvery bare trees, dotted over the rolling hills. The wind carries with it the sounds of birds and the trickling of thaw, and, quite noticeably, a pure sound that is the absence of traffic.

I tell her it's ok.

Devon Iott is a sewing teacher that works for Husqvarna Viking and Pfaff brand sewing machines. She blogs at Miss Make in Nashville, TN with two chickens and a cat.

HOLIDAY LOOKBOOK

Festive

Transform these wardrobe staples into
special pieces with easy upgrades.

Find these patterns at www.seamwork.com

Sparkle and shine this holiday season in festive versions of your favorite Seamwork patterns.

From left to right: an Akita lengthened into a dress, an Aurora tank and Mabel skirt and a Mesa dress.

Mesa lengthened into a midi dress (see tutorial on pg. 37).

Texture adds an interesting detail to the simple lines of Akita, Mesa, and Savannah.

Sparkling neutrals shine and showcase your individual beauty.

COZY

*Brew a cup of tea, and
grab your favorite novel, it's
time to cozy-up indoors.*

Left: Pair the Manila Leggings with the Savannah camisole and the Oslo cardigan for a relaxed and comfortable look. Right: The Akita and Moji make the perfect pair. Choose soft fabric for the perfect secret pajamas.

Fall in love with the great indoors.

Oslo just might be the perfect cardigan. Layer it over your favorite dress, or wear it as longewear.

Find these patterns at www.seamwork.com

CPSIA information can be obtained
at www.ICGtesting.com
Printed in the USA
LVOW05s1108131115

462438LV00004B/4/P

9 780692 573044